SNACKERS

Kick the Junk Food Habit with

SNACKERS

By Maureen & Jim Wallace

MADRONA PUBLISHERS, INC. · SEATTLE

FIRST PRINTING, APRIL 1978
SECOND PRINTING, JUNE 1978

Library of Congress Cataloging in Publication Data

Wallace, Maureen, 1935-
    Snackers: kick the junk food habit.

    Includes index.
    1. Cookery.   2. Snack foods.   3. Food, Junk.
I. Wallace, Jim, 1936-   joint author.
II. Title.
TX652.W25   641.5'3   78-638
ISBN 0-914842-26-9 (USA)
0-88894-193-5 (Canada)

USA

Madrona Publishers, Inc.
2116 Western Avenue
Seattle, Washington 98121

CANADA

Douglas & McIntyre Ltd.
1875 Welch Street
North Vancouver, B.C.

THE ROAD
TO GOOD HEALTH
IS PAVED WITH
GOOD NUTRITION

To:
The Children ...
Whose feet, we hope, will
tread the path that is paved
with good nutrition.

CONTENTS

SNACKERS

BETTER NUTRITION

ADDITIVES

Imitation flavorings, artificial colorings, chemical preservatives: in 1971, manufacturers added an estimated 800 million pounds of chemicals—more than 3,000 different kinds—to our food in order to prolong its shelf life or to alter it cosmetically. This created increased profits for them, not better nutrition for us. Each year the chemical variety increases; today more than 10,000 different additives are used. FDA-approved chemical additives texturize, emulsify, stabilize, preserve, firm, neutralize, flavor, defoam, sweeten, sequester, thicken, unstick, fix, buffer, inhibit, defungus, color and anticake our foods. All are supposedly safe. However, few studies have explored how these chemicals act together to affect our bodies.

Use no artificial flavorings or colorings in your kitchen; select only pure, natural products. Individuals with a history of allergy should know that sensitivity to artificial colorings and flavorings is common and may be responsible for such symptoms as headaches, irritability, fatigue, insomnia and even bizarre emotional outbursts. One federally funded study has confirmed that removing artificial flavorings and colorings from the diets of some children significantly reduces hyperactivity. This remedy has long been advocated by Benjamin Feingold, M.D., Chief Emeritus of the allergy department at San Francisco's Kaiser-Permanente Medical Center.

Avoid foods containing chemical preservatives. Among the worst are nitrates and nitrites. Much has been written lately about the carcinogenic risk in eating these preservatives, which break down in the body to cancer-causing nitrosamines. Inclusion of these additives in your diet:

...interferes with the iodine metabolism of the thyroid gland.

...decreases the blood's ability to carry oxygen.

...depletes the infection-fighting vitamin A supply because the body cannot convert carotene to vitamin A when any amount of nitrate is present.

3

Nitrates and nitrites are present, alone or together, in most cured meats, including hams, bacons, lunch meats and weiners, and in a wide spectrum of other foods. Get used to reading labels.

According to a 1975 Library of Congress Study, the Council on Environmental Quality's Sixth Annual Report and Lon Crosby, M.D., nutritionist for the National Cancer Institute, about 80 percent of all cancer is caused by environmental factors. Dietary causes may be responsible for as much as 30 percent. Many of the cancers being treated today had their beginnings in the food supply of 15 to 20 years ago. There are now far more pollutants in our food and air. What kind of a time bomb are we lighting for our mature years? For our children's adulthood?

SUGAR

Refined sugar has no place in a health-conscious household. Introduce the family to raw, natural, unpolluted honey, molasses, maple syrup and date sugar—pure products available at health food stores.

Refined sugar, the main ingredient in most supermarket snacks, enters the bloodstream rapidly and is used by the body to create quick energy. This sudden sugar onslaught in the blood also warns the pancreas that there is too much sugar out there, which in turn stimulates the production of extra insulin in order to reduce the level of blood sugar. Thus, a dose of refined sugar produces a high-low shock reaction which leaves the individual with less blood sugar than he started with.

Remove refined sugar from your children's diet and you will make them less likely to get cavities—with or without fluoride and sexy toothpaste. Refined white sugar also contributes greatly to obesity. In addition to its other faults, it contains *no* vitamins or minerals.

Sophisticated peering devices are turning up surprising information about refined sugar and overprocessed carbohydrates in the diet and how they relate to cholesterol. These foods create an abnormal sugar-protein molecule. Recent tests with the electron microscope indicate that it is this abnormal molecule which begins the deterioration of the arteries. Cholesterol may then be deposited on a placque of these abnormal molecules, inducing clogging of the arteries.

The level of cholesterol in people's blood has not changed appreciably since the turn of the century, while the rate of death from heart attacks and artherosclerosis problems has risen at a terrifying rate. Research conducted in England indicates that "normal" amounts of refined sugar in the diet increase the stickiness of the blood platelets in some individuals—a precondition to hardening of the arteries. Remove refined sugar and white bread from your diet, while including plenty of whole grains, fresh fruits and vegetables, and the cholesterol will remain free-flowing, able to carry out its necessary functions.

Studies by Jose A. Yaryaru-Tobias, M.D., Director of Research at Manhasset, New York's North Nassau Mental Health Center, indicate that the increasing violence the United States is experiencing may be due, in part, to a disturbance of glucose metabolism triggered by excesses of refined sugars and carbohydrates in such packaged foods as dry breakfast cereals, pizza, spaghetti, white breads and crackers, junk snack foods and soda pop, which form the cornerstones of many American diets.

The average annual consumption of refined white sugar in our country today is 120 pounds per person. That is one pound every three days. And most of it is hidden—it's in our processed and overprocessed foods. Become a label reader. Ingredients must be listed (when they are listed at all) in descending order of volume. Notice how many big food companies are now listing the varieties of sugar in a given product separately, while lumping the beneficial ingredients together. This labeling technique makes the product seem healthful when, really, the reverse is true.

HONEY

Honey is the best sweetener for you to use. It has fewer calories than refined sugar. It contains protein (nine of the ten essential amino acids), phosphorus, potassium, B vitamins and vitamin C.

As a chemically "single (simple) sugar," honey is easier to digest than the "double (complex) sugar" created by refining cane or beet sugar. Honey is principally two natural sugars, 40 percent dextrose and 60 percent levulose. Levulose does not need insulin to be metabolized, thereby avoiding refined sugar's high/low reaction.

Olympic athletes in ancient Greece ate honey for energy and

endurance. Masai warriors of East Africa took no food but honey to thwart fatigue on their long journeys. Over the years, in addition to its sweetening duties, honey has been used to cure hay fever, reduce the effects of drunkenness, ease sore throats and alleviate gastrointestinal complaints. Honey also contains amazing germicidal properties. When used on burns, cuts, abrasions and ulcers, it will stimulate cleansing and promote healing more effectively, less painfully and more cheaply then almost any other substance.

Be certain the honey you choose has not been boiled, filtered or adulterated in any way. Then substitute honey for the sugar in your favorite recipes. To do this use 3/4 cup honey in place of each 1 cup of refined sugar. Then decrease the liquid ingredients by 1/4 cup or increase the dry ingredients by 1/4 cup. After your family's taste buds become accustomed to a more wholesome way of snacking, you can probably reduce the honey using 1/2 cup honey instead of 1 cup refined sugar. If you do, reduce liquid ingredients or increase dry ingredients by another 1/4 cup.

When baking with honey, lower oven temperature 25° because honey makes baked goods brown faster than sugar does. Items baked with honey will also draw moisture from the air, and baked products will become more moist if left uncovered. If you want to retain crispness, store in airtight containers.

For a brown sugar taste, try a molasses and honey mixture. When using honey or molasses, measure the oil in the measuring cup first; the honey or molasses will then slip out easily.

FLOUR

When modern technology replaced the old millstones with steel rollers, it enabled flour mills to remove the germ of the wheat, which spelled the end of good nutrition for flour. Big business then refined the flour, bleached it, sifted it, tried to "enrich" it until all we have left in the supermarket variety is white dust—of little aid to growth or sustenance. The white flour "enrichment" myth is the returning of three nutrients (in one-third the original amounts) of the thirty-three nutrients removed by processing methods. This processing assures a longer shelf life and a more attractive appearance—of the food item, not you—both of which provide increased profits for the processor. Very little consideration is given to the needs of the con-

6

sumer. Whole-grain foods offer a vast spectrum of the B vitamins and the vitamin E necessary for keeping cholesterol free-flowing (not sticking to your artery walls). Stone-ground, whole-grain flour is best for all recipes. Store it in your refrigerator. Try whole wheat pastry flour for your lighter goodies. Check the label on any flour you choose, to be certain that the government-allowed improvers and conditioners have not been added, and that your choice of whole wheat flour has not been bromated or phosphated. If you *must* use white flour, be sure that it is unbleached, thereby avoiding the many chemicals involved in that process. Using unbleached, though, only avoids further chemicalization and does not really provide much nutrition, as the range of B vitamins, calcium, protein and vitamin E are destroyed or removed at the beginning of the white flour process.

Whole Wheat Flour: Substitute whole wheat flour for white flour, cup for cup. If substituting coarsely ground flour, take 2 tablespoons from each cup. In many cases, sifting the whole-grain flour is not necessary. Simply stir lightly with a whisk or a fork. If sifted flour is preferred, always sift (in a single sifter) before measuring. For most recipes, put any bran remaining in the sifter into the measuring cup, then add enough sifted flour to complete the measure. If you are making very light, delicate goodies, save the bran and use it in another recipe or return it to your flour canister.

Bran: A special effort should be made to include some bran in your daily diet. The same milling process which steals many of the nutrients from flour also removes this valuable non-nutritive fiber. Bran and other roughage keep the bowels clean and unblocked. Diverticular disease was identified only a hundred years ago, and then as a rarity. Now, as people include less roughage in their diets, these problems have become so common, so expected, that our stores are stocked with a whole array of laxatives. More Americans each year have a blockage problem so severe that a colostomy becomes necessary—a procedure whereby the inflamed or non-working far end of the bowel is snipped out and the dietary wastes have to be re-routed into a plastic bag. Several documented studies have now shown that this condition can be alleviated and prevented by the addition of bran and other roughage to the diet.

Wheat Sprouts and Malt: An extra-nutritious wheat flour can be made from wheat sprouts. To sprout wheat berries, soak 1/2 cup berries in warm water in a quart jar overnight. Drain off water. Cover the jar mouth with cheesecloth and put in the dark. Gently rinse the berries twice a day in warm water. They are ready to use in 3 or 4 days when the sprouts are at least twice as long as the grain. From 1/2 cup berries you will get about 1 cup sprouts.

For malt, dry the sprouts at a very low temperature (below 140°) in an oven or food dryer. Once the sprouts are thoroughly dry, grind them into flour in your blender or seed mill. This malt can be used most advantageously in any recipe at a ratio of four-parts-whole-wheat-flour to one-part-malt. The sprouting process creates a very high-protein, sweet flour; some decrease in the recipe's sweetener may be necessary.

Variety Flours: Toasted or raw grains, nuts and seeds can be run through a blender to make flour. Sift to remove larger pieces. You can make your own sesame flour, oat flour, rye flour, brown rice flour and sunflower seed flour, to name a few.

High-Protein Powder: Select the high-protein powders made from *natural* ingredients, containing no artificial flavorings, colorings or chemical pollutants, and sweetened, if at all, with raw honey. Check the contents to be certain the powder you choose includes arginine and histidine. Researchers now find that children are unable to manufacture these two amino acids in sufficient quantities to support growth, particularly during periods of stress; it is, therefore, considered necessary to include foods containing these amino acids in the diets of children and some adults.

OIL

Always use cold-pressed oils, usually found in health food sections of supermarkets. Many nationally advertised supermarket oils are made from cottonseed oil (check the label). Cotton is not considered a food crop and is usually sprayed heavily with toxic chemicals which can easily contaminate the oil. Supermarket corn and safflower oils, which may appeal to health-conscious individuals because they are advertised as polyunsaturates, generally contain the common preservatives BHA (butylated hydroxyanisole) and BHT (butylated hydroxytoluene). Use of these antioxidants is strictly forbidden in Great Britain, as is a chemical emulsifier called polysorbate 80, along with other additives such as isopropyl citrate (another antioxidant) and methyl silicone (an antifoaming agent). If you make your purchase in the supermarket, do check the label to be certain the oil you choose is untainted. Your health food store will have a wide variety to choose from, generally free from chemical pollution.

PEANUT BUTTER

Peanut butter used to be made from peanuts and peanut oil. Now, it is likely that the supermarket variety will also include other oils, salt, sugar, chemical "improvers" and be hydrogenated. Check the label to be certain the brand you choose contains only peanuts, peanut oil and, perhaps, salt. Pure peanut butter will have to be stirred before using (the oil tends to separate from the nut paste) and kept in the refrigerator after opening. If you can't find a pure product, consider making your own.

Homemade Peanut Butter: Use roasted or raw peanuts. If you have raw but prefer the taste of roasted, place nuts on baking pan and roast in oven below 200° for a couple of hours. Process shelled nuts in blender or nut grinder until powdery. Gradually add peanut or other oil, a teaspoonful at a time, stopping from time to time to push down the mass from the sides to the center of the container. When it is the consistency you like, add a dash of salt and a smidgen of honey to heighten the flavor. If you like the chunky style, mix in some nut chunks at this point. Store in refrigerator.

Variety Nut Butters: Interesting taste treats can be made from raw or roasted sesame seeds (tahini), cashews, almonds, sunflower seeds, pecans and walnuts. Process as you would peanuts (see above).

MAYONNAISE

By-pass the chemical-laden product from the supermarket and opt for the pure spread found either in health food stores or your own blender.

Homemade Blender Mayonnaise: Place in blender 1 egg, 1/2 teaspoon salt, 1/2 teaspoon dry mustard, 1/4 teaspoon paprika, 1-1/2 tablespoons apple cider vinegar or lemon juice and 1/4 cup oil. Mix at low speed, adding an additional 3/4 cup oil in a slow steady stream. Use spatula to keep mixture moving.

DAIRY PRODUCTS

Milk: Pasteurization, admittedly necessary for the control of bacteria in big commercial dairies, does destroy some of the nutritive value of milk. Certified raw milk, if available in your area, is always the best choice, and has an added advantage of cream at the top of the bottle. If there is a milk digestion problem in your family, substitute:

Nut Milk: Place in blender 1/4 cup chopped nuts and 1 cup fruit juice, water or whey. Process for 3 to 5 minutes until nuts are completely dissolved. Substitute for milk in any recipe.

Butter: Butter is better for you than margarine. Butter has come under attack recently for its alleged role in raising cholesterol levels, but cholesterol is a vitally needed substance. If there is an insufficient supply of cholesterol in the diet, the body will manufacture its own from a variety of food types. Substitute butter or cold-pressed oils (or a mixture of the two) for margarine or shortening in your recipes. For a great spread, whip together equal parts of softened butter and cold-pressed oil with an electric mixer. Pour into ice cube tray or other mold, refrigerate and use instead of plain butter.

Cheese: Most supermarket cheddar cheese is artificially colored. Stick with the white cheeses (swiss, monterey jack, mozzarella) or health food store cheddars.

Eggs: The egg's image has also suffered unfairly in the cholesterol controversy. Eggs contain both unsaturated and saturated fats and are rich in lecithin, the cholesterol emulsifier, as well as in choline, pyridoxine and inositol which are used, along with lecithin, in the prescribed medical treatment of atherosclerosis (hardening of the arteries).

Extensive studies done on split pairs of Irish brothers (one brother of each pair remained in Ireland while the other brother lived in the United States) show that the heart and arteries of the partner in Ireland—where large amounts of milk, butter, cream and eggs were consumed—were very much healthier (10 to 15 body years younger) than those of the brother eating United States foods. Butter, milk, cream and eggs are good foods.

Ice Cream: Many health food stores offer ice cream made from pure cream, eggs, honey and natural fruits. Most supermarket ice creams are a conglomeration of chemicals and sugars. Almost 40 years ago, ice cream manufacturers were granted a two-year exemption from detailing ingredients on labels. They still enjoy this freedom. FDA standards permit the use of a wide range of additives which have been proven harmful to some individuals: antioxidants, buffers, neutralizers, bactericides, surfactants (complex chemical compounds with an action similar to that of detergent), stabilizers, emulsifiers, artificial dyes and imitation flavors. Why not investigate the Creams and Custards section of this book for an easy, healthful alternative?

Yoghurt: Yoghurt can be substituted for milk, cream or sour cream in many recipes. Yoghurt contributes B vitamins, calcium and protein instead of fat and calories to the finished product. In addition, it is reputed to be an excellent intestinal cleanser, allowing the beneficial intestinal flora to flourish. Do select the unflavored kind (made with whole milk, if you can find it) and carefully read the label. Pass it by if you see artificial color or flavor, tartaric acid, potassium sorbate or sodium caseinate listed as ingredients. If you get ambitious, you might even make your own yoghurt. Then you will *know* what it contains.

Easy Thermos Yoghurt: For a one-quart Thermos, heat 3-1/2 cups milk to almost boiling; let cool a bit. Add 1/2 cup yoghurt (for starter) to lukewarm milk; stir well to eradicate lumps. Pour mixture into wide-mouthed Thermos bottle. Let sit (quietly, with no hits, knocks or jiggles) for 4 to 6 hours. Refrigerate if you will use it within a week. Freeze it to keep it for several months. Save 1/2 cup yoghurt to start your next batch.

Yoghurt Cream Cheese: At the end of the 4 to 6 hours (see Easy Thermos Yoghurt), before refrigerating, place colander lined with three layers of cheesecloth in a bowl. Pour yoghurt into colander; let drip for 5 minutes. Tie the four corners of the cheesecloth together and hang over sink faucet; let drip for 6 to 8 hours. Remove cheese from cheesecloth and refrigerate. Use in any cream cheese recipe.

Whey, the drippings in the bowl, can be used in almost any recipe, measure for measure, as a substitute for water or milk. It will impart sweetness, so a decrease in the recipe sweetener may be necessary. If you have no other use for the whey, use it to water your plants.

FRUIT

Whenever possible, choose organically grown, unsprayed fruit. The contaminants on the skin of the supermarket variety can be partially neutralized by washing with a solution of 1/4 cup inexpensive distilled white vinegar and a dishpanful of water. White vinegar works better than apple cider vinegar. It is estimated that this method will remove up to 85 percent of the poisons on the surface of fruit. Even better is to use water and a bit of biodegradable soap for the first washing. Then swish in vinegar water and rinse. Use this method for cleaning vegetables as well as fruit.

Dried Fruit: Most of the dried fruits found in supermarkets are dried by artificial dehydration rather than by the sun. Any fruit with a light, bright color is almost certain to have been treated with sulfur dioxide (creamy apples, orange apricots, golden raisins). Almost all dried fruits are fumigated during storage or importation. Sorbic acid is sometimes put in (as a preservative) as is corn syrup (as a texture improver); the label will divulge these unnecessary additions. That's your cue to keep on searching. Growing popularity of dried fruit is expanding the selection. In many areas now, dried bananas, pineapple and strawberries are available, as well as the old favorites. If you have access to a home food dryer (keep the temperature below 140°) or a sunny location, why not try your hand at drying your own?

Apples: This fruit is not difficult to dry at home. Light color can be retained by dipping before drying in a mixture of orange and lemon juice; honey can also be included in this dip for a special flavor.

Apricots: When these are sun-dried, they are usually a little tough and hard to chew. If you like them softer and more pliant, pour boiling water over the dried fruit and soak for half an hour. Save the water for baking or cooking.

Dates: Since these are one of the most popular dried fruits, you have a variety of choices. There are several brands without unnecessary additives; check the labels.

Prunes: Several brands are routinely subjected to a lye bath. The FDA does not require that this process be reported on the label. You may be able to obtain a more natural product in a health food store.

Carob: Substitute carob powder for cocoa in equal measure. Substitute 3 tablespoons carob powder plus 2 tablespoons water, milk or whey for each square of baking chocolate. Carob is sweeter than chocolate or cocoa, so a decrease in recipe sweetener may be necessary.

Coconut: Unsweetened, raw coconut—generally found only in health food stores—is better than the overprocessed sweetened variety.

Lemon, Lime or Orange Rind: Place the peel of organically grown, unsprayed fruit (including the white part which contains bioflavonoids) in the blender; process at high speed until rind is grated. Store in covered container in refrigerator. This mixture can be substituted in any recipe for store-bought grated rind. Substitute it for extract by using 1-1/2 teaspoons grated rind for 1 teaspoon extract. If you are unable to obtain unsprayed fruit, skip the rind and use extract for flavoring.

Pumpkin Purée: Instead of using canned pumpkin (which may contain sugar), turn your Halloween jack-o-lantern into a treat. Wash the outside skin. Cut pumpkin into pieces, removing any parts that were burned by the candle. Place pumpkin pieces in steamer. Pour boiling water over and steam until tender. After the pumpkin is steamed, peeling is a great deal easier. Put peeled pieces through a ricer and use in any recipe calling for cooked or canned pumpkin.

NUTS AND SEEDS

Whenever practical, purchase raw seeds and nuts and roast and salt them at home. Commercial processors, including those who sell to health food stores, for financial considerations must use the same oil (and there is no way of knowing what *kind* of oil) for many batches. In addition, they generally use too much salt. These same ingredients—processed at home where there is control over the type of oil, a check on its purity and a chance to use sea salt—can contribute to a nutritionally superior product.

Salt

It is true that iodized salt has prevented generations of Americans from getting goiter problems. But today iodized salt from the supermarket also contains additives which are harmful rather than healthful. Sea salt, which contains iodine naturally, and kelp flakes combined with sea salt should be used by a health-conscious family.

A dam built with inferior materials may look all right and may hold up well enough under normal conditions. But when unexpectedly heavy rains fall and the water pressure mounts, it will crumble under the stress.

Our way of life today is filled with stress, emotional and physical. Isn't it a good idea to be sure that the 60 trillion cells in your body are supplied with the best materials available—not inferior or just average—but the kind of materials that will build a structure able to stand up to an onslaught of unexpected pressure?

Recent studies have indicated that one of the major causes of alcoholism may be poor nutrition. In one experiment reported in the *Journal of the American Dietetic Association*, rats fed a diet much like that of many American teenagers developed a craving for alcohol, while rats fed wholesome foods preferred water. When the diets were reversed and the rats on junk food were put on a sound, balanced diet, they lost their interest in alcohol, while the other rats, switched from their healthful diet to junk food, began tippling. Teenage alcoholism is increasing at a frightening rate. What would happen if we could switch some teenagers from junk food to a healthful, balanced diet? Dr. Roger Williams of the University of Texas has said that "no one who follows good nutritional practices will ever become an alcoholic."

The road to health is paved with good nutrition. And we should all make the effort to put our children on that road and keep them on it. It isn't difficult, but it does call for a conscious decision to eliminate the all-too-prevailing junk food from their diet and to make use of available healthful, natural ingredients. Take your first step with the snack foods that follow. You can provide your children with treats without harming their bodies. The child you save may be your own.

BARS & SQUARES

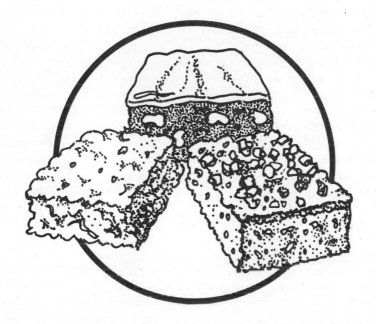

ALMOND SQUARES

1-1/2 cups whole wheat flour
1/4 cup soy flour
2 teaspoons baking powder
1/2 cup oil

1-1/2 cups honey
2 eggs
2 teaspoons almond extract
1 cup raw sesame seeds

Stir together flours and baking powder; set aside. Mix oil and honey, beat in eggs, one at a time, add extract and combine with flour mixture. Stir in sesame seeds. Spread into greased 11 × 7-inch pan. Bake at 350° for 25 to 30 minutes. Cool in pan and cut into squares.

BOUNTY BARS

3/4 cup peanut butter
1/4 to 1/2 cup honey
1 tablespoon milk

1 well-beaten egg
3/4 cup rolled oats
1/2 cup shredded coconut

Cream honey and peanut butter; add milk and egg; mix well. Add remaining ingredients. Pat into lightly oiled 10-inch square baking pan (mixture should be about 1/2-inch deep). Bake at 350° for 10 to 15 minutes.

BROWNIES

1 cup oil
2/3 cup honey
4 beaten eggs
1 cup peanut flour

5 tablespoons rye (or
   whole wheat) flour
1 cup carob powder
1 cup chopped nuts
2 teaspoons vanilla

Mix oil with honey; add eggs and set aside. Whisk together peanut flour, rye or whole wheat flour and carob powder; combine with egg mixture. Add nuts and vanilla. Spread batter evenly into 9-inch square baking dish. Bake at 325° for 30 minutes. Remove from oven and cool 10 minutes. Cut into squares.

CRANWICH

1/2 cup butter
1/2 cup honey
2 eggs

1/2 teaspoon vanilla
2-1/2 cups whole wheat flour
1-1/2 cups cranberry relish
(your own favorite or
recipe on page 86)

Mix butter and honey, blend in eggs and vanilla. Add flour and mix well; chill. Roll dough, half at a time, on lightly floured surface, to a 16 × 9-inch rectangle. Cut into three 16 × 3-inch strips. Spread 1/2 cup cranberry relish down center of one strip. Fold 16-inch edges to the middle and join by pressing together lightly. Cut into 2-inch bars. Place, seam side down, on ungreased baking sheet. Repeat with remaining strips. Bake at 375° for 12 to 15 minutes until lightly browned.

FANTASMO

1 cup raisins
1 cup wheat germ
1/2 cup high-protein powder
1/2 cup powdered milk
1 tablespoon brewer's yeast
(optional)
2 teaspoons cinnamon
1/4 teaspoon each
allspice and nutmeg

1/2 cup sunflower seeds or
chopped nuts
1 cup chopped wheat sprouts
(sprouted from 1/3 cup grain)
1/4 cup oil
2 tablespoons blackstrap
molasses
2 teaspoons vanilla
1/2 cup raisin water
2 well-beaten eggs

Soak raisins overnight (save soak water). Mix dry ingredients, seeds or nuts, wheat sprouts and drained raisins. Combine oil, molasses, vanilla and raisin water. Add to dry ingredients and mix well. Gently fold in eggs. Pour into 11 × 7-inch baking pan lined with waxed paper. Bake at 350° for 40 to 50 minutes. Remove paper and cut promptly.

JUICE BARS

2 tablespoons butter
1/4 cup honey
2 eggs
1 tablespoon orange juice
   concentrate
1 teaspoon vanilla

1 cup whole wheat flour
1/4 cup soy flour
1 cup shredded coconut
1 can (15 oz.) crushed
   pineapple in juice
3/4 cup chopped nuts

Cream butter and honey; add eggs, juice and vanilla. Combine flours and add gradually to creamed mixture, blending thoroughly. Using wooden spoon, add coconut, pineapple and nuts. Spread into oiled 13 × 9 × 2-inch baking pan. Bake at 350° for 45 minutes until nicely browned. Cool before cutting.

LEILANI STACKS

1/2 cup honey
1 cup butter
1 teaspoon vanilla

1/4 teaspoon salt
1-3/4 cup whole wheat flour
1/4 cup soy flour

---

1 can (15 oz.) unsweetened
   crushed pineapple, with juice
1/2 cup honey
2 egg yolks

2 tablespoons cornstarch
1/4 teaspoon salt
1 tablespoon fresh lemon juice
2 teaspoons ground lemon rind

For crust: cream honey, butter, vanilla and salt. Whisk together flours and add all at once to butter mixture; mix until crumbly. Pat two-thirds of the mixture into the bottom of ungreased 11 × 7-inch baking pan. Set aside. *For filling:* combine pineapple, honey, egg yolks, cornstarch and salt in saucepan. Cook over medium heat, stirring constantly, for 5 minutes. Turn heat to low and continue cooking and stirring until mixture is thick and clear. Add lemon juice and rind. Spoon mixture onto the crumb combination in baking pan. Sprinkle the remainder of the crumb mixture over the top. Bake at 325° for 50 minutes or until golden brown. Cool slightly before cutting into squares.

MOLASSES SQUARES

1 cup any combination of dried
   fruit, pitted and chopped
   (consider raisins, dates,
   figs, apples, apricots)
1/2 cup molasses
1/4 cup high-protein powder
1/4 cup oat flour

1/2 cup wheat germ
1/4 cup wheat bran
2 cups chopped nuts
2 tablespoons oil
Just enough grape juice
   to make thick batter

Mix all ingredients together well; spread into greased 8-inch square baking pan. Bake at 300° for 30 to 40 minutes or until firm. Cut into squares immediately but allow to cool before removing from pan.

OAT BARS

3 eggs
3/4 cup honey
1/2 cup oil

2 teaspoons vanilla
4 cups rolled oats
finely chopped nuts

Beat eggs. Blend in honey, oil and vanilla with rolled oats. Pour into two oiled and floured 8-inch square pans. Sprinkle nuts on top and bake at 350° for 10 to 15 minutes. Cool slightly before cutting into bars.

PRUNE PAWS

1/2 cup whole wheat flour
1 teaspoon baking powder
1/2 teaspoon salt
2 tablespoons high-
   protein powder

2 eggs
1/2 cup honey
1 teaspoon vanilla
1 cup chopped nuts
1 cup pitted, chopped prunes

Whisk together flour, baking powder, salt and high-protein powder. Beat eggs and honey until foamy. Add to flour mixture and stir in vanilla, nuts and prunes. Put into greased 8-inch square baking dish. Bake at 325° for 40 minutes. Cut into bars and cool in the pan.

SCRUMPTIOUS SQUARES

2 eggs
1 cup honey
1/4 cup oil
2/3 cup wheat germ

1/3 cup high-protein powder
1/2 teaspoon salt
1/2 cup chopped nuts

Beat together eggs, honey and oil. Combine wheat germ, high-protein powder, salt and nuts; add to honey mixture. Spread batter into oiled 8-inch square baking dish. Bake at 350° for 30 minutes. Cut into squares while still warm.

SESAME SCRIGGLES

2 beaten eggs
1/3 cup tahini
   (sesame-seed butter,
   see page 9)
1/2 cup honey
1 cup chopped nuts
1 cup rolled oats

1/4 cup bran
1/4 cup wheat germ
1/2 cup finely shredded
   coconut
1/4 cup sesame seeds
1 cup raisins

Combine eggs, tahini and honey; add remaining ingredients. Spread into oiled 9-inch square baking dish. Bake at 350° for 20 minutes. Cut into squares and remove to cooling rack.

TRIPLE-DECKER TREATS

3/4 cup molasses
3/4 cup oil
1-3/4 cup whole wheat flour

1/4 cup soy flour
1-3/4 cups rolled oats
1/4 cup bran

1/3 cup honey
3 tablespoons cornstarch
1/2 cup warm water (or whey)

2 tablespoons lemon juice
2-1/2 cups any combination
of chopped dried fruit

Blend first six ingredients together forming crumb mixture. Press one-half mixture into lightly oiled 12 × 8-inch baking dish. Place second set of six ingredients in saucepan. Cook over low heat, stirring constantly, until mixture thickens. Cool and pour over crumb mixture in baking dish. Top with remaining half of crumb mixture. Bake at 400° for 25 minutes. When slightly cooled, cut into bars.

YUMMIES

3 eggs, well beaten
3/4 cup honey
3/4 cup whole wheat flour
1/4 cup soy flour
1/2 teaspoon salt
1 teaspoon baking powder

1 cup chopped, pitted dates
1 cup chopped nuts
1/2 cup shredded coconut
1/4 cup wheat germ
1/4 cup bran

Mix eggs with honey. Blend in dry ingredients. Add nuts and dates. Spread into well-oiled 9-inch square baking dish. Bake at 350° for 30 minutes. Cut into squares while still warm.

CAKES & CHEESECAKES

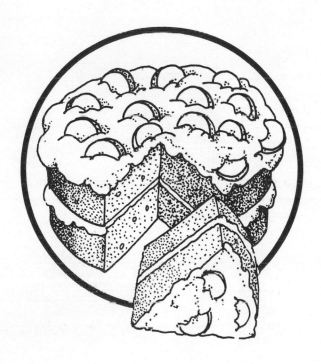

Apple Cake

1/4 cup oil
3/4 cup honey
1 egg
3/4 cup whole wheat flour
1/4 cup soy flour
1/4 cup bran

1/2 teaspoon salt
1 teaspoon vanilla
1 teaspoon cinnamon
2 cups thinly sliced apples
1/2 cup chopped nuts
1/2 cup raisins

Combine all ingredients; batter will be dry. Press into oiled 9-inch round cake pan and bake at 375° for 45 minutes.

Applesauce Cake

1-3/4 cups whole wheat flour
1/4 cup soy flour
3 teaspoons baking powder
1 teaspoon cinnamon
1/2 teaspoon each allspice
and nutmeg
1/4 teaspoon each cloves
and salt

2 eggs
3/4 cup honey
1/2 cup oil
2 cups hot applesauce
1 cup chopped, pitted dates
3/4 cup chopped nuts

Whisk together flours, baking powder, spices and salt. Mix together eggs, honey, oil and applesauce; add to flour mixture. Stir in dates and nuts. Pour batter into oiled 9-inch square baking pan. Bake at 350° for 50 minutes. Let cool 10 minutes and frost right in pan.

BEET CAKE

4 medium beets
3 eggs
3/4 cup honey
1 cup oil
1/2 cup carob powder

1-1/2 cups whole wheat flour
1/4 cup soy flour
2 teaspoons baking powder
1/4 teaspoon salt
1 teaspoon vanilla

Steam beets until tender; peel, quarter and place in blender. Add eggs, honey and oil; blend until beets are pureed. Whisk together carob powder, flours, baking powder and salt. Add blender ingredients and vanilla. Pour into greased, floured 9-inch tube pan. Bake at 350° for 50 to 60 minutes.

CAKE ROLL-UP

5 egg whites
2 teaspoons lemon juice
5 egg yolks
1/2 cup honey

1 teaspoon vanilla
1/2 cup whole wheat flour
1/4 cup soy flour

Beat egg whites until soft peaks form; add lemon juice and beat until stiff. Beat egg yolks until thick; add honey slowly while continuing to beat. Mix in vanilla. Fold yolks into whites. Sprinkle flours onto mixture and fold together carefully. Pour into 10 × 15-inch jelly-roll pan, oiled and lined with oiled waxed paper. Bake at 375° for 12 minutes or until cake starts to pull away from edges of pan. Tip from pan onto long strips of waxed paper. Remove baked paper from bottom of cake and roll cake up in waxed paper strips. Cool slightly. Unroll and coat cake with whipped cream, custard or frosting.

CAROB-BANANA CREAM

1-3/4 cups whole wheat flour
3/4 cup soy flour
2 teaspoons baking powder
1 teaspoon salt
1/2 cup oil
1-1/4 cups honey
3 large eggs
1/2 cup carob powder mixed
   with 1/2 cup hot water

2/3 cup yoghurt
1 teaspoon vanilla
1 carob candy bar (8 oz.)
1/4 cup water
1 cup whipping cream
4 ripe bananas, sliced

Whisk together flours, baking powder and salt. Mix oil and honey; beat in eggs, carob, yoghurt and vanilla. Mix dry ingredients into wet ones. Pour into three 9-inch round cake pans, greased and lined on the bottom with waxed paper. Bake at 350° for 25 minutes. Cool in pans before removing. Melt carob candy bar with water in top of double boiler. Cool; fold in whipped cream. Cover the bottom cake layer with one-third cream mixture. Place half the banana slices evenly on cream. Repeat on second layer; no bananas for top layer. Refrigerate immediately.

CAROB CAKE

3/4 cup whole wheat flour
1/4 cup soy flour
1/2 cup carob powder
1-1/2 teaspoons cinnamon
6 eggs, separated

1/3 cup softened butter
1/2 cup honey
1/3 cup water (or whey)
2 teaspoons vanilla

Combine dry ingredients. Beat egg yolks with butter and honey; add water and vanilla. Mix with dry ingredients. Fold in stiffly beaten egg whites. Pour into greased 9-inch spring-form pan. Bake at 350° for 45 minutes. Frost when cool.

CAROB-DATE RECTANGLE

4 large eggs, separated
1/4 cup honey
1 teaspoon vanilla
1 teaspoon salt
1/4 cup carob powder

1/4 cup soy flour
1/4 cup wheat germ
1 cup pitted, chopped dates
1 cup chopped nuts or seeds

Beat egg yolks until thick; add honey and vanilla. Whisk together salt, carob powder, flour and wheat germ. Fold into egg yolk mixture. Add dates and nuts. Beat egg whites until stiff and gently fold into batter. Pour into oiled 11 × 8-inch baking dish. Bake at 350° for about 20 minutes. May be served warm without icing or frosted when cool.

CAROB-HONEY ROUND

1/2 cup soft butter
1-1/4 cups honey
2 eggs
1/2 cup carob powder
2-1/4 cups whole wheat flour
1/4 cup soy flour

2 teaspoons baking powder
1 teaspoon salt
2/3 cup yoghurt
1-1/2 teaspoons vanilla
1 cup chopped nuts or seeds

Cream butter and honey; add eggs and beat until fluffy. Combine carob powder, flours, baking powder and salt. Add to creamed mixture alternately with yoghurt, beating after each addition. Add vanilla and nuts. Pour into two oiled 8-inch cake pans. Bake at 350° for 30 to 35 minutes. Cool cakes in pans on racks for 5 minutes, then turn out and cool completely. Frost.

CARROT-RAISIN RING

2-1/4 cups whole wheat flour
1/4 cup soy flour
2 teaspoons baking powder
1 teaspoon salt
1-1/2 teaspoons each cinnamon
    and nutmeg

4 eggs
1 cup honey
1 cup oil
2-1/2 cups grated carrots
1 cup raisins
1 cup chopped nuts

Combine flours, baking powder, salt, cinnamon and nutmeg. Beat eggs with honey and oil; add to dry ingredients. Stir in carrots, raisins and nuts. Pour into well-oiled 9-inch tube pan. Bake at 350° for 1 hour and 10 minutes or until top springs back when lightly pressed with fingertip. Remove from oven and cool on wire rack 10 minutes. Loosen sides with metal spatula and remove from pan. Cool and frost.

CARROT-YOGHURT SQUARE

2 eggs
1/2 cup oil
1 cup honey
1/4 cup yoghurt
1-3/4 cups whole wheat flour
1/4 cup soy flour
2 teaspoons baking powder

1/4 teaspoon salt
1-1/2 teaspoons cinnamon
1 cup chopped nuts
1 cup pitted, chopped
    dried fruit
1 cup grated carrots

Beat eggs; add oil, honey and yoghurt. Combine flours, baking powder, salt and cinnamon; add to egg mixture. Stir in nuts, dried fruit and carrots. Mix well. Spread into greased 9-inch square pan. Bake at 350° for 45 minutes. Cool and frost.

HONEY CAKE

2 eggs
1-3/4 cups honey
2 tablespoons oil
1 cup yoghurt
3 cups whole wheat flour
1/4 cup soy flour

2-1/2 teaspoons baking powder
1 tablespoon ground lemon rind
1/4 cup finely chopped almonds
1/4 teaspoon each cinnamon,
    cloves and nutmeg

Beat eggs; add honey, oil and yoghurt. Combine remaining ingredients; add to egg mixture. Pour into oiled 9-inch tube pan. Bake at 350° for 45 minutes. Cool and ice.

Honey Spice Cake

2 cups honey
3/4 cup oil
1-1/4 cups juice (or whey)
1 cup raisins
1 teaspoon each cinnamon,
 nutmeg, cloves, allspice
 and baking powder

2-3/4 cups whole wheat flour
1/4 cup soy flour
2 teaspoons baking powder
1 teaspoon salt
3 cups chopped nuts

Mix honey, oil, juice, raisins, cinnamon, nutmeg, cloves, allspice and baking powder together in saucepan. Stir and cook over low heat 5 minutes. Combine flours, baking powder and salt. Pour honey mixture into flour mixture and blend well. Stir in nuts. Pour into oiled, floured 9-inch tube pan. Bake at 350° for 1 hour and 15 minutes. Cool and frost.

Pineapple Cake

5 eggs, separated
1/2 cup honey
1-1/2 cups wheat germ
3 cups ground nuts

1 can (20 oz.) unsweetened
 crushed pineapple,
 including juice

Beat egg yolks until light; add honey and beat again. Add wheat germ and ground nuts; beat. Stir in pineapple. Fold in stiffly beaten egg whites. Pour into two greased 8-inch cake pans or one greased 8-1/2 × 12-inch baking pan. Bake at 325° for 30 minutes. Cool and frost.

Pious Angel's Food

1-2/3 cups egg whites (12 or
 13) at room temperature
1/2 teaspoon salt
1-1/2 teaspoons cream of tartar
1 teaspoon vanilla

1 teaspoon almond extract
2/3 cup honey
1 cup whole wheat pastry flour
2 tablespoons cornstarch

Beat egg whites until foamy; sprinkle with cream of tartar and salt and beat until stiff but not dry. Gradually mix in honey and flavorings. Sprinkle flour and cornstarch over egg mixture and fold in gently but quickly. Place in ungreased 10-inch tube pan; draw spatula through dough to eliminate air pockets. Bake at 375° for·35 to 40 minutes. Remove from oven, invert pan immediately and cool thoroughly before attempting to remove cake. To use egg yolks, try Maple Freeze, page 69 (6 yolks), or Brown Rice Imperial, page 66 (4 yolks). Extra yolks can also be stirred into your favorite soup with a wire whisk to give it added body and nutrition.

PROTEIN CAKE

7 eggs, separated
1/2 cup honey
1/2 cup high-protein powder
2 cups finely ground nuts

pinch of salt
1 teaspoon vanilla
1/2 teaspoon nutmeg

Beat egg yolks with honey. Gradually add high-protein powder and nuts, then salt, vanilla and nutmeg. Fold this mixture into stiffly beaten egg whites. Pour into greased 9-inch tube pan. Bake at 325° for 1 hour. Cool in pan.

THE SQUARE CARROT

6 eggs, separated
3/4 cup honey
1-1/4 cups grated carrots
1-1/4 cups chopped nuts

3/4 cup whole wheat flour
1/4 cup soy flour
1 teaspoon cinnamon

Beat egg yolks with honey until light and creamy. Add carrots, chopped nuts, flours and cinnamon. Fold this mixture into stiffly beaten egg whites. Pour into 8-inch square baking dish. Bake at 350° for 45 minutes. Cool and ice.

YOGHURT BONANZA

1 cup softened butter
3/4 cup honey
2 eggs
1 cup carob powder
1 cup yoghurt
3/4 cup whole wheat flour

1/4 cup soy flour
1/4 cup wheat germ
1 teaspoon salt
2 teaspoons baking powder
1 cup chopped nuts
1/2 cup fruit preserves

Cream butter with honey until light and fluffy. Add eggs, carob and yoghurt; beat well. Add dry ingredients and nuts and beat again. Pour into well-buttered 8-inch baking dish. Spoon preserves over the top of batter. Bake at 350° for 45 to 60 minutes.

YOUR CHOICE CAKE

1 cup applesauce or mashed
    banana or cooked pumpkin
1/2 cup honey
1/2 cup oil
1/2 cup chopped nuts
1-1/2 cups whole wheat flour

1/4 cup soy flour
2 teaspoons baking powder
1 teaspoon vanilla
1 teaspoon cinnamon
1/2 teaspoon each cloves,
    ginger, salt

Combine applesauce, banana or pumpkin with honey and oil. Add remaining ingredients. Blend well and spoon into greased and floured 8-inch square baking dish. Bake at 350° for 40 minutes. Remove from pan to cool. Frost.

ALMOND CHEESECAKE

1/2 cup ground almonds
3/4 cup wheat germ

1 tablespoon honey
1/4 cup melted butter

---

2 cups (16 oz.) cream cheese
1 cup yoghurt
3 tablespoons whole wheat flour
1 cup honey

4 eggs, separated
1/2 teaspoon almond extract
1 teaspoon ground lemon rind

For crust: combine almonds, wheat germ, honey and melted butter; press into the bottom of a 9-inch spring-form pan. *For filling:* cream together cream cheese, yoghurt, whole wheat flour and honey until light and fluffy. Add egg yolks, one at a time; then add almond extract and lemon rind. Fold into stiffly beaten egg whites. Pour into crust. Bake at 325° for 1 hour and 15 to 30 minutes or until lightly browned and firm.

COTTAGE CHEESECAKE

1/4 cup cornstarch
1 cup yoghurt
2 cups cottage cheese
1 tablespoon lemon juice

1/2 cup honey
2 teaspoons vanilla
4 eggs, separated
1 crumb crust (pages 99-101)

In a blender, dissolve cornstarch in yoghurt; add cottage cheese and blend until smooth. Add lemon juice, honey and vanilla. Beat egg yolks in bowl until thick; add cheese mixture and beat well. Beat egg whites until stiff; fold into cheese mixture. Pour into 10-inch spring-form pan which has been lined with crumb crust. Bake at 300° for 50 minutes or until center is firm. Turn off oven and leave cake inside with door closed for about 1 hour or until cool. Loosen sides of pan and remove cake. Refrigerate overnight.

EGG CHEESECAKE

8 eggs
4 cups cottage cheese
1 cup yoghurt
3 tablespoons lemon juice
1 tablespoon lemon extract

1 cup honey
1/4 cup whole wheat flour
1/4 cup wheat germ
1 teaspoon cinnamon
1 crumb crust (pages 99-101)

Beat eggs until thick and creamy; add remaining ingredients and blend thoroughly. Pour into a 9-inch spring-form pan which has been lined with crumb crust. Bake at 300° for 1 hour. Turn off oven (do not open door) and leave cake inside for 1-1/2 hours more. Refrigerate overnight.

PEANUT CHEESECAKE

1/2 cup ground peanuts	1 tablespoon honey
3/4 cup wheat germ	1/4 cup melted butter

2 cups (16 oz.) cream cheese	4 eggs, separated
1 cup yoghurt	1/2 cup peanut butter
3 tablespoons whole wheat flour	1 teaspoon each orange juice and salt
1 cup honey	

For crust: combine peanuts, wheat germ, honey and butter; press into the bottom of a 9-inch spring-form pan. *For filling:* cream together cream cheese, yoghurt, flour and honey until light and fluffy. Add egg yolks, one at a time; then add peanut butter, orange juice and salt. Fold into stiffly beaten egg whites. Pour into above crust. Bake at 325° for 1 hour and 15 to 30 minutes or until lightly browned and firm.

PIECRUST CHEESECAKE

2 cups cottage cheese	1/4 cup honey
1 cup (8 oz.) cream cheese	1 9-inch unbaked granola pie shell (page 100)
2 eggs	
2 teaspoons vanilla	

Mix all ingredients until smooth. Pour into pie shell. Bake at 350° for 45 minutes or until firm. Refrigerate overnight.

PUMPKIN CHEESECAKE

1/2 cup ground walnuts	1 tablespoon honey
3/4 cup wheat germ	1/4 cup melted butter

2 cups (16 oz.) cream cheese
1 cup yoghurt
3 tablespoons whole wheat flour
1 cup honey
4 eggs, separated
1 teaspoon lemon juice

1 cup puréed pumpkin
1 teaspoon cinnamon
1 teaspoon nutmeg
1/2 teaspoon ginger
1/4 teaspoon cloves

For crust: combine walnuts, wheat germ, honey and butter and press into the bottom of a 9-inch spring-form pan. *For filling:* cream together cream cheese, yoghurt, flour and honey until light and fluffy. Add egg yolks, one at a time; then add lemon juice, pumpkin, cinnamon, nutmeg, ginger and cloves. Fold into stiffly beaten egg whites and pour into above crust. Bake at 325° for 1 hour and 15 to 30 minutes or until firm and lightly browned.

SPICE CHEESECAKE

2/3 cup wheat germ
2/3 cup whole wheat flour
1/4 teaspoon each allspice
and nutmeg

1/2 teaspoon cinnamon
3-1/2 tablespoons butter
2/3 cup cashew meal
2 tablespoons honey

6 eggs
1 cup yoghurt
3 cups (24 oz.) cream cheese
1/3 cup orange or apple
juice concentrate

1 teaspoon each vanilla
and cinnamon
1/4 teaspoon each allspice,
nutmeg, cloves, ginger
1-1/3 cups honey

For crust: mix together wheat germ, flour, allspice, nutmeg and cinnamon. Cut butter into flour mixture as for pastry dough. Add cashew meal and honey. Press into bottom and sides of an oiled 9-inch spring-form pan. *For filling:* process remaining ingredients in blender until smooth. Pour into above crust and bake at 300° for 2 hours. Cheesecake should be golden, not brown. Refrigerate immediately for at least 6 hours or overnight.

CANDY SNACKS

CANDY BASICS

The ingredients below can be combined in an almost unlimited number of ways to make healthful, nourishing candies. Select ingredients from both the dry and moist categories — additions and flavorings, too, if you like — mix them, and press into square dishes; chill and cut into squares. Or form the mixture into rolls; chill and slice. Or shape into balls; roll in any dry ingredient listed below, wrap individually in waxed paper and chill. The following recipes will get you started. Ready, set, go!

MOIST:
Applesauce
Bananas
Butter
Maple syrup
Honey
Molasses
Nut butters
Oil
Pumpkin purée
Tahini
Peanut butter
Fruit purée

DRY:
Protein powder
Nuts, raw or toasted,
    finely chopped
Cornmeal
Milk, powdered
Brown rice, finely ground
Sunflower seeds, whole or
    finely ground
Wheat germ, raw or toasted
Coconut, unsweetened,
    shredded
Soy grits
Carob powder
Brewer's yeast
Graham cracker crumbs
Chia seeds
Flax, ground
Sesame seeds

ADDITIONS:
Chopped dried
fruit:
    Raisins
    Apples
    Dates
    Figs
    Prunes
    Apricots

FLAVORINGS:
Extracts
Juices
Grated rind

BONZIES

2 large, ripe bananas
1 cup ground nuts
1 tablespoon honey

Mash the bananas; mix in nuts and honey. Form small balls and roll in additional ground nuts or ground seeds.

BUTTERSCOTCH CHEWS

1/2 cup honey
2 tablespoons pure, sweet butter

In small saucepan, simmer butter and honey for about 12 minutes. Pour into very lightly buttered soup bowl; cool. Shape into small balls, put on plate and refrigerate to set. Wrap individually, like taffy, in waxed paper.

CAROB BRITTLE

1-1/4 cups whole, raw almonds
1-1/4 cups honey
1/4 cup carob powder
1 tablespoon water

1/4 cup butter
2 teaspoons baking powder
1 teaspoon vanilla

Coarsely chop almonds; spread in baking pan and roast at 300° for 15 minutes or until lightly browned. Set aside. Mix honey, carob powder, water and butter in heavy saucepan. Bring to a boil, stirring constantly, and continue cooking until syrup reaches 280° on candy thermometer (it's ready if, when dropped into cold water, the syrup separates into hard and brittle threads). Remove roasted almonds to a bowl and lightly oil the baking pan. Remove syrup from heat and quickly stir in baking powder, vanilla and almonds. Pour mixture into baking pan and spread thinly. When cool, break into pieces.

CAROB CLUSTERS—BAKED

1/2 cup warm water
2 tablespoons butter
1/3 cup powdered milk
1/2 cup carob powder

2 tablespoons lecithin granules
1 cup shelled peanuts
  (with skins)
1 cup raisins

Place water, butter, powdered milk, carob and lecithin in blender; process until smooth. Combine peanuts and raisins in mixing bowl; pour carob mixture over; stir to coat well. Spoon clumps of mixture onto lightly oiled baking pan. Starting in cold oven, bake (on middle rack) at 300° for 10 to 15 minutes. Remove and allow to dry for several hours.

CAROB CLUSTERS—REFRIGERATED

1 cup almonds
2 to 2-1/2 cups carob chips
3 tablespoons powdered milk
3 tablespoons oil
3 tablespoons lecithin

1-1/2 cups shredded coconut
1 cup chopped cashews
1 teaspoon salt
2 teaspoons vanilla

Coarsely chop almonds; spread in baking pan and roast at 300° for 15 minutes or until lightly browned. Set aside. In top of double boiler, mix chips, powdered milk, oil and lecithin. Stir over hot, not boiling, water until chips are melted and mixture is smooth. Combine all other ingredients in a bowl and pour melted mixture over. Drop in clumps onto waxed paper. Refrigerate to set.

CAROB-NUT FUDGE

1 tablespoon butter
1/2 cup milk
1-1/4 cups honey

1/4 cup carob powder
1/2 teaspoon salt
1 cup chopped nuts

Melt butter; add milk, honey and carob. Cook slowly, stirring constantly, until mixture boils. Boil gently, stirring occasionally, for 8 minutes. Add salt; remove from heat and beat until creamy. Add nuts; spread into greased 8-inch square dish. Cool. Cut into squares.

CAROB SQUARES

4 tablespoons (4 envelopes)
   unflavored gelatin
1-1/2 cups water or fruit juice
1/4 cup honey

1-1/2 cups carob powder
1 teaspoon vanilla
1/2 teaspoon cinnamon
1/2 cup chopped nuts

Sprinkle gelatin into liquid in saucepan; stir over low heat until gelatin is dissolved. Remove from heat; stir in honey, carob powder, vanilla and cinnamon. Beat until smooth and creamy. Stir in nuts. Spread into 9-inch square dish; chill until firm. Cut into 1-inch squares.

CAROB STIX

1 cup high-protein powder
1/4 cup carob powder
1 cup grated coconut,
   plus extra for coating
3/4 cup honey (more, if necessary)

Combine high-protein powder, carob and 1 cup coconut. Add honey and mix until dry ingredients are moistened. Roll small pieces of mixture in hands to form thin sticks approximately 2 inches long. Roll these in coconut.

CRANAPPLE SQUARES

4 tablespoons (4 envelopes)
   unflavored gelatin
1-1/2 cups cranberry-apple juice (page 128)
1/4 cup honey
1 teaspoon grated orange rind

Sprinkle gelatin over 1 cup juice in saucepan. Stir over low heat until gelatin is thoroughly dissolved. Remove from heat; add honey, remaining juice and orange rind.

Pour into 9-inch square dish; chill. Cut into squares.

DOUBLE-COATED GLOBS

2 cups shelled nuts
5 tablespoons honey
1 tablespoon blackstrap
   molasses
3 tablespoons raisins

sufficient carob powder
   for coating
sufficient sesame seeds
   for coating

Place nuts in blender; grind to a flour. Pour into mixing bowl. Add honey and molasses; mix well. Add raisins and blend until you have a sticky, cohesive mass. Shape into small balls; roll in carob powder. Place on waxed paper. After about 15 minutes, honey will have soaked through carob. Roll balls in sesame seeds. Can be served immediately.

ENERGY BOOSTERS

3 cups wheat germ
1 cup high-protein powder
1 cup honey

1 cup peanut butter,
   sesame seeds or
   finely chopped nuts

Mix wheat germ and high-protein powder; mix honey and peanut butter. Knead the two mixtures together with hands until stiff; form into balls. Roll in seeds or nuts. Wrap individually in waxed paper. Carry a few of these in a pocket or purse for those times when lunch is delayed or cancelled.

FROOTSIE ROLLS

1 cup raw wheat germ
1/4 cup soy grits
1/4 cup high-protein powder
1 cup soy lecithin granules
1/2 cup date sugar
1 cup carob powder
1 cup sunflower meal

1/2 cup honey
1/2 cup oil
2 teaspoons vanilla
1-1/2 cups chopped dates
1 cup raisins
water
1 cup shredded coconut

Combine dry ingredients. Combine honey, oil, vanilla, dates and raisins. Mix dry and wet combinations together, adding just enough water so that you can knead the mixture lightly. Divide into thirds. Sprinkle coconut onto waxed paper. Shape dough into 1-1/2 × 10-inch rolls; coat with coconut and wrap each roll individually in waxed paper. Store in refrigerator. To serve, cut into slices. Great to put in lunch boxes.

GRANOLA FINGERS

3/4 cup honey
1/2 cup peanut butter
2 eggs

1/4 cup butter
1 cup chopped peanuts
3 cups granola (see page 86)

Mix honey and peanut butter in saucepan; beat in eggs, one at a time. Stir over medium heat until mixture boils and leaves sides of pan. Remove from heat and stir in butter. Add peanuts and granola; mix well. Press into oiled 9-inch square pan; refrigerate. Cut into skinny bars.

GREAT FUDGE

1 cup honey
1 cup peanut butter
1 cup carob powder
1 cup sesame seeds
1/2 cup shredded coconut

1/2 cup any combination of
    chopped dried apricots,
    chopped dried apples
    or chopped dates

Heat honey and peanut butter in saucepan; quickly stir in carob powder, then add remaining ingredients. Turn into lightly oiled 9-inch square dish; refrigerate to harden. Cut into squares.

SESAME SEED CANDY

1 cup sesame seeds
1 teaspoon vanilla
honey
nut halves

Process sesame seeds in blender until they become a mass; add vanilla. Knead on a flat surface, working in honey until mixture is the consistency of bread dough. Shape into flat rounds; press nut half on top of each.

SESAME TREATS

1/4 cup finely ground coconut
1/2 cup sunflower seed meal
1/2 cup wheat germ

1/4 cup tahini
1/4 cup honey
1 teaspoon almond extract

Mix all ingredients together. Divide mixture in half; form into two rolls, each approximately 1 inch in diameter. Wrap rolls in waxed paper and store in refrigerator. Slice to serve.

SIMBAS

1 cup dried apricots
1/2 cup nut meats
2-1/2 cups coconut
4 tablespoons lemon juice
Ground nuts for coating

Put apricots, nut meats and coconut through a food grinder. Add lemon juice. Shape into 1-inch balls and roll in ground nuts. Refrigerate.

SPUN SQUARES

1-1/2 cups dried apricots
1-1/2 cups unsweetened
  pineapple juice
5 tablespoons (5 envelopes)
  unflavored gelatin

1 cup honey
1 teaspoon vanilla
1/4 teaspoon ground cloves
1-1/2 cups chopped nuts

Place coarsely chopped apricots and 1/2 cup pineapple juice in blender. Process until coarsely puréed. Combine gelatin and 1 cup pineapple juice in saucepan. Stir over low heat until gelatin is thoroughly dissolved. Remove from heat; add honey, vanilla, cloves and nuts. Stir well and add the apricot mixture. Put in 9 × 12-inch dish and chill until firm. Cut in small squares to serve. If a bit sticky, coat with finely ground coconut. May be made ahead and frozen. Coat with coconut after thawing.

Stuffed Fruties

1 cup raisins
1 cup shredded coconut
3/4 cup combined sunflower
   seeds and nuts
1 tablespoon lemon juice
   (approximately)

dried prunes and
   apricots, pitted
pitted dates, slightly
   cooked and drained

Put raisins, coconut, seeds and nuts through grinder. Blend mixture and lemon juice. Use 1/2 teaspoonful of mix to each piece of fruit in stuffing prunes, apricots and dates. Great for sustained energy as well as the sweet tooth.

Super Snacks

1 cup high-protein powder
1 cup grated coconut
   (plus extra for coating)
3/4 cup honey

Knead ingredients together and shape into peanut-sized globs. Coat with coconut; wrap individually in waxed paper.

Tutti-Frutti

1-1/2 cups dried apricots
1 cup pitted prunes
1-1/2 cups dried apples
2-1/2 cups pitted dates

2-3/4 cups raisins
2 cups nut meats
1/2 cup sunflower seeds
shredded coconut

Pour hot water over apricots; cover; let stand for 30 minutes. Drain (save water for other sweetening or cooking). Force fruits, nuts and seeds through food chopper, alternating fruits and nuts to minimize stickiness. Form into 1-inch balls and roll in coconut.

WHEAT BALLS

1/2 cup softened cream cheese
1 cup sprouted wheat
  (see page 7)
1 cup chopped nuts

1 cup chopped dried fruit
sesame seeds, finely chopped
  nuts or toasted wheat germ
  for coating

Mix cream cheese, sprouted wheat, nuts and dried fruit together until well-blended. Shape into small balls and roll in coating mixture of your choice.

YAHOOS

1-1/2 cups ground sunflower seeds
1 cup pitted, chopped dates
1/4 cup honey

Grind seeds in blender to a fine powder. In bowl, mix dates with 1 cup of seed powder. Add honey and blend until well-mixed. Shape into 1-inch balls and coat with remaining ground seeds.

ZIPPY CASHEWS

1-1/4 cups chopped raw cashews
2 tablespoons honey

Combine 1 cup nuts and honey; mix until well-blended. Shape into 1-inch balls and coat with remaining cashews. Chill until firm.

COOKIES

Almond Melts

2 cups unblanched almonds
3/4 cup honey
2 egg whites
1 teaspoon vanilla
2/3 cup shredded coconut

Pulverize almonds in blender, 1/4 cup at a time. Sift to remove any large pieces. Gradually blend honey into ground almonds. In mixing bowl, whip egg whites until stiff. Slowly beat in almond mixture until thoroughly combined. Add vanilla. Shape into 1-inch balls, roll in coconut and place on oiled baking sheet. Flatten with fork. Bake at 375° for 10 to 12 minutes or until golden.

Anise Cookies

1-3/4 cups brown rice flour
1/4 cup sesame meal
1/2 cup oil
1/4 teaspoon salt

1/4 cup honey
1 slightly beaten egg
1/2 teaspoon vanilla
1 tablespoon ground anise seed

Combine ingredients and mix well. Form into balls, place on lightly oiled baking sheet and flatten with fork. Bake at 350° for 15 minutes.

BREAKFAST BABIES

1 cup soy flour
1/2 cup brown rice flour
1/2 cup sunflower seed meal
1/2 cup wheat germ
1/2 teaspoon salt
1/2 cup rolled oats
1/2 cup raisins

1/2 cup apple juice
2 eggs
1/4 cup oil
1/2 cup honey
1/4 cup blackstrap molasses
1/2 cup peanut butter

Combine dry ingredients and raisins. Combine wet ingredients and add to dry mix. Blend well. Drop by spoonfuls onto oiled cookie sheet. Bake at 350° for 10 to 12 minutes.

BUNNY MUNCHIES

1/2 cup honey
1/2 cup butter
2 beaten eggs
1 teaspoon vanilla
1 cup whole wheat flour
1/4 cup soy flour
2 teaspoons baking powder

1/4 teaspoon salt
1/2 teaspoon cinnamon
1/2 cup oat flakes
1/2 cup wheat germ
1 cup shredded carrots
1/2 cup raisins
1/2 cup nuts

Cream butter and honey; add eggs and vanilla and mix well. Combine dry ingredients; stir into egg mixture. Add carrots, raisins and nuts; stir until well-mixed. Drop by spoonfuls onto oiled cookie sheet. Bake at 375° 10 to 12 minutes until delicately browned.

BUTTER STAMPS

1 cup butter
1/3 cup honey
1-1/2 cups whole wheat
   pastry flour

1/4 cup sesame flour
1/4 teaspoon salt
1 teaspoon almond extract

Cream butter and honey. Add almond extract, then flours and salt. Chill dough. Form into 1-inch balls and place on oiled cookie sheet. Stamp with cookie stamp. Bake at 350° for 12 to 15 minutes.

CAROB CHEWS

1-1/2 cups carob chips
1/2 cup butter
1/2 teaspoon salt
3 eggs

1/2 cup honey
1-1/4 cups rolled oats
1 teaspoon vanilla

Melt chips over hot, not boiling, water. When melted, remove from heat; stir in butter and salt. Beat eggs and honey; add carob mixture, oats and vanilla; mix well. Drop by spoonfuls onto oiled cookie sheet. Bake at 375° for 8 to 10 minutes.

CAROB CHIP COOKIES

1/2 cup softened butter
1 cup honey
2 slightly beaten eggs
2 cups whole wheat flour

1/4 cup soy flour
2 teaspoons baking powder
1 cup chopped nuts
1 cup carob chips

Cream butter and honey; add eggs; add remaining ingredients and mix well. Chill dough. Drop by spoonfuls onto oiled cookie sheet. Bake at 350° for 10 to 12 minutes.

CAROB CUTOUTS

1/2 cup butter
3/4 cup honey
1/3 cup milk (or whey)
2 eggs
6 tablespoons carob powder

4 cups whole wheat pastry flour
1/4 cup soy flour
4 teaspoons baking powder
1/2 teaspoon salt
1 teaspoon vanilla

Cream butter and honey; add milk; add eggs, one at a time, beating after each addition. Combine dry ingredients; add slowly to creamed mixture. Add vanilla; mix well. Chill until firm. Roll out 1/8-inch thick on lightly floured board. Cut into shapes; place on oiled baking sheet. Bake at 400° for 8 to 10 minutes.

CASHEW DREAMS

1/2 cup oil	1 cup whole wheat flour
1/2 cup honey	1 teaspoon salt
1 egg	1 teaspoon baking powder
1 teaspoon vanilla	1 cup rolled oats
3/4 cup cashew butter	
(see page 9)	

Combine oil, honey, egg and vanilla; add cashew butter. Combine dry ingredients and add to egg mixture. Drop by spoonfuls onto oiled cookie sheet. Bake at 350° for 10 minutes. Allow to cool slightly before removing to cooling rack.

CHEESE NUTS

1/2 lb. grated cheddar cheese	dash of cayenne
1 cup whole wheat flour	3 to 4 tablespoons milk
3 tablespoons oil	1/3 cup finely chopped nuts
1/4 teaspoon salt	

Purchase cheese from health-food store, making certain there has been no artificial coloring added. Mix cheese, flour, oil, salt and cayenne until crumbly. Add milk and nuts. Form into 1-inch balls. Place on oiled cookie sheet and bake at 350° for 20 minutes.

COCO-NOATS

2 eggs	1/2 cup whole wheat flour
1/4 cup oil	1/2 cup bran
1/4 cup honey	1-1/2 cups rolled oats
1 teaspoon almond extract	1/2 cup shredded coconut
1/4 cup powdered milk	1/2 cup chopped nuts
1/4 cup high-protein powder	1/2 cup raisins

Beat eggs; add oil, honey and almond extract and mix well. Combine dry ingredients and add to egg mixture. Stir in coconut, nuts and raisins. Drop by spoonfuls onto oiled cookie sheet. Bake at 375° for 20 minutes.

COWBOY COOKIES

1 cup oil
1/2 cup peanut butter
3/4 cup honey
1 cup molasses
2 eggs
2 cups whole wheat flour
1/4 cup soy flour

2 cups rolled oats
1 cup wheat germ
2 teaspoons baking powder
1 cup raisins
1 cup shredded coconut
1 cup chopped peanuts

Mix together oil, peanut butter, honey and molasses; and add eggs, one at a time. Combine dry ingredients, raisins, coconut and peanuts, and add to creamed mixture. Drop by spoonfuls onto oiled cookie sheet. Bake at 375° for 10 to 12 minutes.

CREAM CHEESE PRESSED COOKIES

1/2 cup butter
1 cup (8 oz.) cream cheese, softened
3/4 cup honey
1 egg yolk
1 teaspoon vanilla

1 teaspoon grated orange rind
2-3/4 cups whole wheat pastry flour
1/4 cup soy flour
1/2 teaspoon salt

Beat together butter, cheese and honey; add egg yolk, vanilla and rind. Combine dry ingredients and stir into creamed mixture. Fill cookie press and form cookies on ungreased baking sheet. Bake at 350° for 12 to 15 minutes.

GRANOLA GRUNDIES

1 egg
1 cup oil
3/4 cup honey
1 teaspoon vanilla

1-1/2 cups whole wheat flour
1/4 cup soy flour
1 teaspoon baking powder
3 cups granola (see page 86)

Beat egg; add oil, honey and vanilla. Combine flours and baking powder; add to egg mixture. Blend thoroughly. Stir in granola. Drop by spoonfuls onto ungreased baking sheet. Bake at 350° for 12 minutes.

MINCEMEAT MOUNDS

2-1/4 cups whole wheat flour
1/4 cup soy flour
1 teaspoon baking powder
1/2 teaspoon salt
2 cups bran flakes

2 eggs
1/2 cup oil
3/4 cup honey
1 cup mincemeat

Combine dry ingredients; set aside. Beat together eggs, oil and honey; add to dry ingredients. Stir in mincemeat. Drop by spoonfuls onto oiled cookie sheet. Bake at 350° for 12 minutes.

MOLASSES FROGS

1/2 cup molasses
2 tablespoons oil
1 cup grated raw carrots
1-1/2 cups whole wheat flour
1/2 cup soy flour
2 tablespoons brewer's yeast
2 tablespoons high-protein
   powder

1 teaspoon nutmeg
1/2 teaspoon cinnamon
1/4 cup orange juice
1 cup chopped nuts
1 cup chopped dates

Combine molasses and oil. Add other ingredients; mix well. Drop by spoonfuls onto oiled cookie sheet. Slightly flatten with fork. Bake at 350° for 12 minutes.

OATMEALERS

1/2 cup wheat germ
1/2 cup soy flour
2-1/2 cups rolled oats
1½ tsp 1 tablespoon baking yeast
1/2 teaspoon salt
3/4 cup chopped peanuts

1/2 cup raisins
2/3 cup molasses
1/3 cup oil
2 eggs
1/2 cup juice
1 teaspoon vanilla

Combine dry ingredients, peanuts and raisins. Beat together molasses, oil, eggs, one at a time, juice and vanilla. Add to dry ingredients. Drop by spoonfuls onto oiled cookie sheet. Bake at 375° for 10 to 15 minutes.

OAT-NANAS

1 egg
3/4 cup honey
3/4 cup oil
1 cup mashed bananas
1/2 cup whole wheat flour
1/2 cup wheat germ
1/2 cup bran

1 teaspoon baking powder
1 teaspoon salt
1 teaspoon cinnamon
1/2 teaspoon nutmeg
1-3/4 cups rolled oats
1 cup chopped nuts
1 cup raisins

Beat egg; add honey and oil. Mix in bananas. Combine dry ingredients; add to banana mixture. Stir in nuts and raisins. Drop by spoonfuls onto ungreased cookie sheet. Bake at 375° for 15 to 20 minutes.

PEANUTIES

1-1/2 cups peanut butter
1/4 cup oil
3/4 cup honey
1 egg
3/4 cup milk

1-3/4 cups whole wheat flour
1/4 cup soy flour
1 cup wheat germ
1-1/2 teaspoons baking powder
1/2 teaspoon salt

Mix peanut butter, oil, honey, egg and milk. Combine dry ingredients; moisten with peanut butter mixture. Shape into 1-inch balls. Place on ungreased cookie sheet; flatten with fork dipped in flour, making crisscross marks on tops. Bake at 350° for 10 to 15 minutes.

POPPY SEED SLICES

1 cup butter
3/4 cup honey
2 eggs
1 teaspoon vanilla
2-3/4 cups whole wheat flour
1/4 cup soy flour

1 teaspoon baking powder
1 teaspoon salt
2 teaspoons cinnamon
1 teaspoon ginger
1/2 cup poppy seeds

Mix butter and honey; add eggs, one at a time. Add vanilla. Combine dry ingredients; mix with creamed mixture. Stir in poppy seeds. Shape into 2-inch diameter roll; wrap in waxed paper; refrigerate overnight. Cut into 1/4-inch slices. Bake on ungreased cookie sheet at 375° for 10 to 12 minutes.

PUMPKIN COOKIES

3/4 cup honey
1 cup pumpkin, puréed
   (see page 13)
1/2 cup oil
1 teaspoon vanilla
2 cups whole wheat flour
1/4 cup soy flour

2-1/2 teaspoons baking powder
1/2 teaspoon salt
1 teaspoon cinnamon
1/2 teaspoon nutmeg
1/4 teaspoon ginger
1 cup raisins
1/2 cup chopped nuts

Mix honey, pumpkin, oil and vanilla. Combine dry ingredients; add to pumpkin mix. Stir in raisins and nuts. Drop by spoonfuls onto oiled cookie sheet. Bake at 350° for 12 to 15 minutes.

RAISIN COOKIES

1-1/2 cups raisins
3/4 cup water
1 cup honey
3/4 cup oil
3 eggs
3 cups whole wheat flour

1/4 cup soy flour
1 cup wheat germ
1/2 cup powdered milk
1/2 teaspoon salt
1 teaspoon cinnamon

Simmer raisins and water in saucepan 20 minutes. Combine honey and oil; beat in eggs. Combine remaining ingredients and add to honey mixture. Drain raisins (save water for cooking or sweetening), add and mix well. Drop by spoonfuls onto oiled cookie sheet. Bake at 350° for 10 to 12 minutes.

RICE-A-ROONIES

4 cups whole wheat pastry flour
2 cups brown rice flour
1 cup corn meal
1 tablespoon cinnamon
1 teaspoon ginger
1 teaspoon cloves

1 teaspoon salt
1/2 cup ground sesame seeds
3/4 cup oil
1/2 cup molasses
2 cups apple juice or cider

Combine dry ingredients and seeds. Combine all liquids except 1 cup of the apple juice. Combine wet and dry ingredients. Add enough of the remaining apple juice to make a soft dough. Wrap in waxed paper and chill overnight. Roll on floured surface to 1/2-inch thickness. Cut with cookie cutters. Bake on oiled cookie sheet at 375° for 12 to 15 minutes.

SESAME SEED TWISTS

4 cups whole wheat pastry flour
1 cup sesame flour
3/4 cup soy flour
1 tablespoon baking powder
1 cup butter

3/4 cup honey
4 eggs
2 teaspoons vanilla
1 tablespoon water
sesame seeds

Combine flours and baking powder; set aside. Cream butter and honey; add 3 eggs and vanilla. Beat until light and fluffy. Mix flour and cream mixtures until just combined. Shape a heaping table-spoonful of dough into 6-inch long rope; fold rope in half and twist together with 2 turns. Repeat until all dough is used. In small bowl, whisk remaining egg with water. Brush each cookie with egg mixture; dip, egg side down, into a quantity of sesame seeds. Place on ungreased cookie sheet. Bake at 350° for 15 to 20 minutes. Cool completely on a rack. Store in air-tight container.

SLICED OATNUTS

1/4 cup peanut butter
1/4 cup butter
1/2 cup honey
1 egg, beaten
1/2 teaspoon vanilla

1 teaspoon orange extract
1 cup oatmeal
1 cup whole wheat flour
1/4 cup chopped nuts

Mix together peanut butter, butter and honey. Add egg, vanilla, orange extract, dry ingredients and nuts. Shape into a roll about 2 inches thick. Wrap in waxed paper and chill 4 hours or overnight. Cut into 1/8-inch slices with sharp knife. Place slices on ungreased cookie sheet. Bake at 350° for 8 to 10 minutes or until edges are lightly browned. Remove from pan immediately and cool on rack.

SPICED SLICES

1/2 cup butter
2/3 cup honey
1 egg
1-3/4 cups whole wheat flour
2 tablespoons wheat germ

1 teaspoon cinnamon
1 teaspoon nutmeg
1/2 teaspoon ginger
1/2 teaspoon cloves

Beat butter and honey together until smooth. Beat in egg. Add flour, wheat germ and spices; stir until smooth. Shape dough into 2 logs (about 8 inches long each); wrap in foil and refrigerate or freeze until needed (at least one hour). When ready to bake, cut into 1/4-inch slices and place on ungreased baking sheet. Bake at 350° for 10 to 12 minutes.

SUNSHINE DROPS

1 cup oil
1 cup honey
1 egg
1/4 cup juice
1-3/4 cups whole wheat flour

1/4 cup soy flour
1/4 teaspoon salt
1/4 cup high-protein powder
1 cup chopped nuts
1 cup chopped dried apricots

Combine oil and honey. Beat in egg and juice. Combine dry ingredients, nuts and apricots. Mix with egg mixture until just smooth. Drop by spoonfuls onto ungreased cookie sheet. Bake at 325° for 10 to 15 minutes.

TAHINI TREATS

1/2 cup honey
6 tablespoons tahini (sesame
  seed butter, see page 9)

1/2 cup chopped nuts
1/2 teaspoon cinnamon
1-1/2 cups rolled oats

Stir honey and tahini together; add nuts. Mix cinnamon and oatmeal flakes; blend with honey mixture. Drop by teaspoonfuls onto oiled cookie sheet. Bake at 350° for about 10 minutes or until edges are brown. Chopped apples, raisins or dates may be added.

WHEAT GERM CRITTERS

1/4 cup oil
1 cup honey
2 tablespoons molasses
2 eggs
2 teaspoons vanilla
1/4 cup soy flour
1/4 cup high-protein powder

1/2 cup whole wheat flour
1/4 cup powdered milk
1/2 cup chopped dates
1/2 cup chopped nuts
1 teaspoon salt
1-1/2 cups wheat germ
2 cups oatmeal

Combine oil, honey and molasses; add eggs, one at a time, beating well after each addition. Add vanilla. Combine flours, high-protein powder and powdered milk. Add dates, nuts, salt, wheat germ and oatmeal. Stir wet ingredients into dry ingredients and blend well. Drop by teaspoonfuls onto lightly oiled cookie sheet. Bake at 350° for 10 minutes.

WHEAT GERMS

1/2 cup oil
3/4 cup honey
2 eggs
1 teaspoon almond extract
1/4 cup high-protein powder

1/4 cup powdered milk
1 cup wheat germ
1 cup oatmeal
1/2 teaspoon salt
1/3 cup toasted soy grits

Combine oil and honey; add eggs and almond extract. Combine protein powder, powdered milk, wheat germ, oatmeal and salt. Add dry ingredients to wet ingredients; mix well. Stir in soy grits.

Drop by teaspoonfuls onto lightly oiled cookie sheet. Bake at 350° for 10 to 12 minutes.

ZUCCA COOKIES

1 egg
1/2 cup oil
3/4 cup honey
1 cup grated zucchini
1-1/2 cups whole wheat flour
1/4 cup soy flour

1/4 cup high-protein powder
1 teaspoon cinnamon
1/2 teaspoon cloves
1/2 teaspoon salt
1 cup chopped nuts
1 cup raisins

Beat egg until light and fluffy. Add oil, honey and zucchini; mix well. Combine flours, protein powder, spices and salt; add to zucchini mixture. Stir in nuts and raisins. Drop by spoonfuls onto oiled baking sheet. Bake at 375° for 12 to 15 minutes.

CREAMS & CUSTARDS

APPLE CREAM

1/4 lemon,
   cut into 3 pieces
2 cups applesauce
1 cup (8 oz.) softened
   cream cheese

1/2 cup honey
1 teaspoon vanilla
1 cup whipping cream

Place lemon in blender; process 30 seconds. Add 1 cup apple-sauce, cream cheese and honey; blend. Add vanilla and second cup of applesauce and process until very smooth; stir in cream. Pour into shallow pan and freeze until solid about 1 inch in from edge all around the pan. Scrape back into blender; blend smooth. Freeze until firm enough to serve or freeze solidly and let stand at room temperature about 10 minutes before serving.

BERRY SOUFFLÉ

2 cups berries
3 tablespoons honey
2 tablespoons lemon juice
1 cup whipping cream
whole berries for garnish

Process berries in blender on high speed until smooth. Add honey and lemon juice. Reserve 1/2 cup berry mixture in small bowl. Whip cream and fold gently into remaining berry mixture. Chill 2 hours. Top each serving with dab of reserved berry puree and garnish with one whole berry.

BROWN RICE IMPERIAL

2 cups cooked, short grain
  brown rice
1-1/2 cups milk
2 tablespoons (2 envelopes)
  unflavored gelatin

1 cup orange juice
1 tablespoon grated orange rind
3/4 cup honey
4 egg yolks, slightly beaten
1 cup heavy whipped cream

Combine rice and milk in saucepan; cook over medium heat about 20 minutes or until all milk is absorbed. To soften, sprinkle gelatin on orange juice; stir in orange rind. Combine honey and egg yolks in top of double boiler. Stir over hot (not boiling) water until mixed. Add gelatin mixture and rice; cook until slightly thickened. Cool, chill and fold in whipped cream. Pour into 6-cup mold. Chill several hours before serving.

BROWN RICE PUDDING

2 eggs
2 cups milk
1/3 cup honey
1 teaspoon vanilla

1-1/2 cups cooked, short grain
  brown rice
dash nutmeg
1/2 cup plumped raisins

Beat eggs; add milk, honey, vanilla, rice, nutmeg and raisins. Pour into 1-quart baking dish and dust with more nutmeg. Bake at 350° for 1 to 1-1/2 hours. Serve chilled or warm, plain or topped with fruit.

CAROB ICE CREAM

3 eggs, separated
3/4 cup honey
3 cups whipping cream
4 tablespoons carob powder
1-1/2 teaspoons vanilla

Beat egg yolks until thick; add honey gradually. Blend in cream, carob and vanilla. Freeze until firm. Place in chilled bowl and add egg whites, which have been beaten stiff and dry; beat entire mixture until smooth. Return to freezing tray. Freeze until firm.

CAROB MINT ICE CREAM

Add 1 teaspoon mint extract to above recipe.

CITRUS SHERBET

2 tablespoons (2 envelopes)
  unflavored gelatin
1/4 cup water
1/2 cup honey (adjust to
  sweetness of fruit)

1 cup freshly squeezed lime,
  lemon, orange or
  tangerine juice
1 cup whipping cream

Soften gelatin in water in saucepan over low heat. Stir and heat until thoroughly dissolved. Add honey; blend in citrus juice. Freeze until fairly firm. Whip cream until stiff and blend with frozen mixture until smooth. Freeze. Whip mixture again and spoon into serving dishes. Place in freezer. Remove 15 minutes before serving.

COLORED CREAM

2 tablespoons (2 envelopes)
  unflavored gelatin
1/2 cup fruit juice
2 cups yoghurt

1-1/2 cups any fruit or berry
1-1/2 teaspoons vanilla
2 tablespoons honey
crushed nuts or coconut

Soften gelatin in fruit juice in blender. Blend until gelatin is thoroughly dissolved. Add yoghurt, 3/4 cups fruit, vanilla and honey. Process until smooth. Stir in remaining fruit. Pour into a 3-quart mold. Chill until set. Unmold and garnish with crushed nuts or coconut.

EGG CUSTARD

3 beaten eggs
1/3 cup honey
1-1/2 cups hot milk
1/2 teaspoon salt
1 teaspoon vanilla

Beat together all ingredients. Pour into 5 or 6 custard cups or a 1-1/2-quart baking dish. Bake at 425° for 10 minutes, then 375° for 15 to 20 minutes.

EGG MOUSSE

2 tablespoons (2 envelopes)
  unflavored gelatin
1 cup pineapple juice
8 egg yolks
3/4 cup milk

2 teaspoons vanilla
1/4 teaspoon salt
8 egg whites
3/4 cup honey
nutmeg

Sprinkle gelatin over juice in saucepan. Stir over low heat until dissolved. Beat egg yolks until thick; add milk, vanilla and salt. Pour in melted gelatin and mix gently. Beat egg whites until foamy. Drizzle honey into them, beating after each drizzle until egg whites peak. Fold into yolk mixture. Chill well in 3-quart mold or individual serving dishes. Dust with nutmeg.

FRUIT MUSH

1 egg
1 cup fruit juice
1 banana

2 cups cut-up fruit
1 tablespoon honey
nutmeg

Put all ingredients into blender and process until the consistency of thick applesauce. Dust with nutmeg.

GLAZED CARMEL CUSTARD

3 eggs
1/4 cup molasses, plus extra
1/4 teaspoon salt

1 teaspoon vanilla
2 cups scalded milk
finely chopped nuts

Beat eggs slightly; add molasses, salt and vanilla. Stir in milk. Place a teaspoon of molasses into each of 5 6-ounce custard cups. Pour milk mixture into cups over molasses. Place cups in shallow pan. Fill pan with hot water to a depth of 1 inch. Bake at 325° for 40 to 45 minutes. Serve, unmolded, lightly sprinkled with nuts.

GRANOLA CUSTARD

1 cup granola (see page 86)
3 cups milk
3 eggs
3/4 cup honey

1 teaspoon vanilla
1 teaspoon salt
1 teaspoon cinnamon

Combine ingredients; chill several hours or overnight. Stir and pour into lightly oiled 1-1/2-quart baking dish. Bake at 350° for 1 hour and 30 minutes.

HONEY ICE YOGHURT

1 cup yoghurt
1/2 cup fresh fruit purée
1 tablespoon lemon juice

1/4 cup honey
1/4 teaspoon salt
2 egg whites

Mix yoghurt with fruit; add lemon juice, honey and salt. Freeze in ice tray until firm. Whip until smooth. Beat egg whites until stiff; fold into yoghurt mixture. Freeze again.

MAPLE FREEZE

2/3 cup maple syrup
6 egg yolks
1/4 teaspoon salt
2 cups whipped cream

Beat together syrup, yolks and salt in top of double boiler. Cook over simmering water until mixture begins to thicken. Cool and fold in whipped cream. Freeze.

PECAN CUSTARD

3 eggs
2 cups milk
1 cup molasses

1/4 cup melted butter
1 teaspoon vanilla
1 cup chopped pecans

Beat eggs with molasses; add remaining ingredients. Pour into ungreased 1-quart baking dish. Bake at 375° for 15 minutes; reduce heat to 325° and bake 25 to 30 minutes longer.

PUMPKIN CUSTARD

1-3/4 cups pumpkin, cooked
  and puréed (see page 13)
1/4 cup cooked brown rice
1/4 cup raisins
1/4 cup honey
1/4 cup molasses
2 eggs

1-1/4 cups orange juice
1 tablespoon soy flour
1/4 teaspoon each cinnamon,
  ginger, cloves
1/4 teaspoon salt
1/2 teaspoon nutmeg

Process all ingredients in blender until well blended. Pour into lightly oiled 1-1/2-quart baking dish. Place this dish in larger pan partly filled with hot water. Bake at 450° for 15 minutes, then 350° for 45 minutes.

TRY!

PUMPKIN PUDDING

1-1/2 cups milk
1/2 cup powdered milk
1-1/2 cups cooked pumpkin
1/2 cup molasses
3 slightly beaten eggs

1 teaspoon each salt
  and cinnamon
1/2 teaspoon each ginger
  and cloves
1 teaspoon vanilla
1 cup chopped nuts

Blend milk and powdered milk together in saucepan. Stir in pumpkin, molasses, eggs, salt, cinnamon, ginger and cloves. Cook until mixture thickens. Cool slightly and add vanilla and chopped nuts.

WHEY GELATO

1 tablespoon (1 envelope)
   unflavored gelatin
1/2 cup powdered milk
2 cups whey (or skimmed milk)

1/2 cup honey
2 teaspoons lemon juice
2 unbeaten egg whites

Mix together gelatin and dry milk in saucepan. Stir in whey. Stir over low heat until gelatin is dissolved. Remove from heat; stir in honey and lemon juice. Pour into ice tray and freeze until firm. Turn into chilled bowl, add egg whites and beat, at high speed, until smooth and fluffy. Freeze.

ZIPPY GELATIN

1 tablespoon (1 envelope)
   unflavored gelatin
1/4 cup water
1/4 cup honey

1 teaspoon vanilla
juice of one lime
apple juice
1 cup whipping cream

Mix gelatin and water in saucepan; stir over low heat until gelatin is dissolved. Remove from heat; add honey and vanilla. Place lime juice in 1-cup measuring cup and fill with apple juice. Add juice mixture to pan. Refrigerate to jell slightly. Whip cream and fold into jelled mixture. Refrigerate until firm.

DESSERT BREADS

ANISE LOAF

3-3/4 cups whole wheat flour
1/4 cup soy flour
5 teaspoons anise seeds
4 teaspoons baking powder
1 teaspoon salt
1/2 cup chopped dates

2 tablespoons oil
1/4 cup honey
2 beaten eggs
1-1/2 cups warm water
(or whey)

Whisk together dry ingredients. Add dates. Beat together remaining ingredients; add wet mix to dry. Stir just enough to moisten. Bake in 2 greased 5 × 9-inch loaf pans at 350° for about 30 minutes or until browned and pulling away from sides of pans.

APPLE BREAD

1-1/2 cups whole wheat flour
1/4 cup soy flour
1/4 cup wheat germ
1/2 teaspoon salt
1 teaspoon baking powder
2 cups apples,
    coarsely chopped

1 cup chopped nuts
3 tablespoons yoghurt
2 teaspoons lemon juice
1 teaspoon grated rind
1/2 cup honey
2 large eggs
1/2 cup oil

Whisk together dry ingredients. Add apples and nuts. Beat together remaining ingredients; add wet mix to dry. Stir just enough to moisten. Bake in 2 greased 5 × 9-inch loaf pans at 350° for 45 minutes.

APPLESAUCE LOAF

2 cups applesauce (or 2
   chopped apples and
   1/4 cup apple juice)
2 tablespoons oil
2 eggs
3/4 cup honey

1-3/4 cups whole wheat flour
1/4 cup soy flour
1 teaspoon each baking powder,
   salt, cinnamon
1 cup chopped nuts

Put applesauce in blender (or process apples and apple juice until consistency of thick sauce). Blend in oil, honey and eggs. Combine flours, baking powder, salt and cinnamon. Stir together wet and dry ingredients; add nuts. Pour into 2 greased 5 × 9-inch loaf pans and bake at 350° for 1 hour.

BANANA NUT BREAD

1/3 cup oil
2/3 cup honey
1/4 teaspoon grated lemon rind
2 beaten eggs
4 to 6 ripe bananas

1-3/4 cups whole wheat flour
1/4 cup soy flour
2-1/2 teaspoons baking powder
1 cup chopped nuts

Blend oil, honey and lemon rind. Beat in eggs and bananas. Add blended dry ingredients and stir in nuts. Pour into greased 5 × 9-inch loaf pan and bake at 350° for 1 hour.

BANANA OAT BOAT

1-3/4 cups oat flour
1/4 cup sesame flour
1/4 cup high-protein powder
3/4 cup powdered milk
3/4 teaspoon baking powder
1-1/4 teaspoons cream
   of tartar

1/2 teaspoon salt
2 eggs
1 cup (or more) mashed bananas
1 tablespoon vanilla
1/3 cup oil
1 cup chopped peanuts
1/2 cup sunflower seeds

Whisk together dry ingredients. Beat together eggs, bananas, vanilla and oil. Mix wet with dry ingredients; add nuts and seeds. Pour into greased and floured 5 × 9-inch loaf pan; bake at 350° for 45 minutes.

BANANA RICE LOAF

1 cup millet flour (or meal)	2 eggs
1 cup rice flour	1/2 cup oil
1 teaspoon baking powder	1/2 cup honey
1/2 teaspoon salt	1 cup mashed bananas

Whisk together dry ingredients. Beat together eggs, oil, honey and bananas. Mix wet with dry ingredients; pour into greased 5 × 9-inch loaf pan. Bake at 350° for 45 minutes.

CARROT BREAD—PLAIN

3/4 cup oil	1 cup wheat germ
2 eggs	1-1/4 cup whole wheat flour
3/4 cup honey	1 teaspoon baking powder
1 cup grated carrots	1/2 teaspoon salt
1/2 cup soy flour	1 teaspoon nutmeg

Mix oil, eggs and honey; add carrots, then remaining ingredients. Mix well and pour into 2 greased 5 × 9-inch loaf pans. Bake at 350° for 45 to 60 minutes.

CARROT BREAD—FANCY

2 eggs, separated	3 tablespoons carob powder
1/2 cup raisins	1-1/2 teaspoons cinnamon
3/4 cup whole wheat flour	2 teaspoons grated orange rind
1/4 cup soy flour	1/4 teaspoon salt
1/2 cup bran	1 cup grated carrots

Beat egg whites until stiff and set aside. Put raisins in a cup and fill with hot water; pour into large mixing bowl. Stir together and add remaining ingredients. Fold egg whites into mixture and bake in greased 5 × 9-inch loaf pan at 350° for 55 minutes.

CORNBREAD LOAF

3 eggs (separated)
2 cups corn meal
1 teaspoon salt
1/4 cup high-protein powder
1/4 cup powdered milk
2 teaspoons baking powder

1/2 cup wheat germ
2 tablespoons honey
1 cup yoghurt
2 tablespoons oil
chopped nuts

Beat egg whites until stiff; set aside. Whisk together dry ingredients. Beat together egg yolks, honey, yoghurt and oil. Mix wet with dry ingredients; fold in egg whites. Pour into greased 5 × 9-inch loaf pan and top with chopped nuts. Bake at 400° for 30 minutes.

CRANBERRY LAYERED LOAF

1 cup granola
1/4 cup chopped nuts
1/4 cup melted butter
1-1/2 cups cranberry relish

Mix granola, nuts and melted butter. Lightly oil a glass loaf pan. Press 1/3 of the crumb mixture on bottom of pan. Spread 1/2 of the cranberry relish over crumbs. Repeat and top with remaining crumbs. Place in refrigerator for 4 hours or overnight.

GINGERBREAD LOAF

1 egg
3/4 cup molasses
1/3 cup oil
1-1/2 cups whole wheat flour
1 teaspoon baking powder

2 teaspoons cinnamon
2 teaspoons ginger
1/4 teaspoon salt
1/2 cup hot water

Mix egg, molasses and oil; add to combined dry ingredients. Add hot water. Bake in greased 5 × 9-inch loaf pan at 350° for 30 minutes. Cool 10 minutes before removing from pan.

GRAPE-NUT BREAD

1/2 cup Grape-Nuts
2 teaspoons baking powder
1 cup yoghurt
1 egg
1/2 cup honey

2 tablespoons oil
1-1/4 cups whole wheat flour
1/4 cup soy flour
1 teaspoon salt

Mix Grape-Nuts, baking powder and yoghurt; store in refrigerator for 1 hour. Mix egg, honey and oil. Whisk together flours and salt; add to egg mixture. Stir in refrigerated mixture and pour into greased 5 × 9-inch loaf pan. Bake at 350° for 1 hour.

HONEY LOAF

1/2 cup softened butter
1 cup honey
2 beaten eggs
1 cup whole wheat flour
1/4 cup soy flour

1 teaspoon baking powder
1/2 teaspoon salt
1 cup chopped nuts
1 cup raisins

Cream together butter and honey; add eggs. Combine dry ingredients and add to egg mixture. Stir in nuts and raisins. Pour into greased 5 × 9-inch loaf pan and bake at 350° for 45 minutes.

PEANUT BUTTER LOAF

1/2 cup softened butter
1/2 cup peanut butter
1/4 cup molasses
3 eggs
1/2 cup honey
1 teaspoon vanilla
1/2 cup yoghurt

1-3/4 cups whole wheat flour
1/4 cup soy flour
dash salt
2 teaspoons baking powder
2 tablespoons high-protein
   powder

Mix butter, peanut butter and molasses. Add eggs, one at a time. Beat until fluffy. Stir in honey, vanilla and yoghurt. Mix dry ingredients and add to peanut butter mixture. Bake in greased 5 × 9-inch loaf pan at 325° for approximately 1 hour.

PROTEIN NUT BREAD

1 cup whole wheat flour
1 cup soy flour
1 cup wheat germ
2/3 cup high-protein powder
4 teaspoons baking powder
1 teaspoon salt
1 teaspoon cinnamon

1/4 teaspoon each
  nutmeg and ginger
2 eggs
1/4 cup oil
3/4 cup honey
1 cup yoghurt
1 teaspoon vanilla
2 cups chopped nuts

Whisk together dry ingredients. Beat together wet ingredients. Mix wet with dry ingredients; add nuts. Pour into 2 well-greased 5 × 9-inch loaf pans and bake at 350° for 45 to 60 minutes.

PUMPKIN BREAD

1-1/4 cups honey
3/4 cup softened butter
2 eggs
2 cups puréed pumpkin
  (see page 13)
2-3/4 cups whole wheat flour

1/4 cup soy flour
2 teaspoons baking powder
1 teaspoon each nutmeg,
  cinnamon, cloves
1 cup raisins
1 cup coarsely
  chopped nuts

Cream honey and butter; add eggs and blend. Stir in pumpkin. Combine dry ingredients and mix with pumpkin mixture. Fold in raisins and nuts. Bake in 2 greased 9 × 5-inch loaf pans at 350° for 30 to 45 minutes.

ZUCCA BREAD

3 eggs
3/4 cup oil
1-1/2 cups honey
3 cups grated zucchini
3 teaspoons vanilla
1 teaspoon almond extract
2-3/4 cups whole wheat flour
1/4 cup soy flour
2 teaspoons baking powder

1 teaspoon salt
2 teaspoons cinnamon
1 teaspoon nutmeg
1/2 to 1 cup rolled oats
    (quantity varies according
    to moisture content of
    zucchini)
1 cup chopped nuts

Beat eggs until light and fluffy; add oil, honey, zucchini, vanilla and almond extract. Mix well. Combine flours, baking powder, salt and spices; add to zucchini mixture. Stir in oats and nuts. Pour batter into 2 greased and floured 5 × 9-inch loaf pans. Bake at 325° for approximately 1 hour. Will freeze nicely.

MISCELLANEOUS TREATS

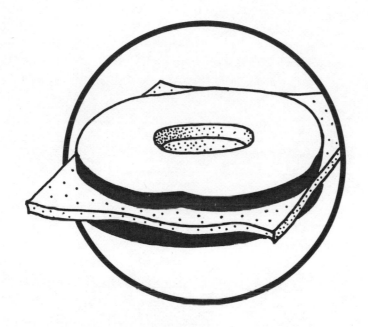

Apple Bowl

1 chopped apple
1 grated apple
2 tablespoons ground
   sunflower seeds

2 tablespoons raisins
1 tablespoon wheat germ
1 tablespoon honey

Combine all ingredients and serve.

Applesauce—Raw

1/4 cup unsweetened apple
   or pineapple juice
approximately 2 cups cut-up
   apples (if unsprayed, leave
   skins on; otherwise peel)

1/2 cup raisins
1/4 teaspoon cinnamon
honey to taste

Pour juice into blender, add apples and process. Add raisins and cinnamon; process again. Taste. If necessary, add honey. Can be frozen.

Banana Friz

3 bananas

Peel bananas; place on plate; cover with waxed paper. Freeze until solid. Remove from paper and plate and place in freezer bag. Return to freezer until needed.

CRANBERRY RELISH—RAW

1 lb. fresh cranberries,
  washed and drained
1 medium apple, peeled
  and cored
1 cup unsweetened crushed
  pineapple, drained

1/2 cup honey
1/4 teaspoon ginger
1/4 teaspoon ground cloves

Put cranberries and apple through food grinder or, if using blender, add pineapple juice. Add drained pineapple; blend in honey and spices. Refrigerate for at least 6 hours before serving.

GRANOLA—RAW

1/2 cup honey
1/2 cup oil
1 tablespoon molasses
2 cups rolled oats
1 cup wheat germ
1 cup shredded coconut

1/2 cup almonds
1/2 cup pecans or walnuts
1 tablespoon high-protein
  powder
1/2 teaspoon kelp
2 tablespoons carob powder

Combine honey, oil and molasses. Combine all other ingredients in large mixing bowl. Add honey mixture to oat mixture. Mix until blended. Serve for breakfast; sprinkle over applesauce; combine with yoghurt for pudding.

GRANOLA—TOASTED

6 cups rolled oats
  (or any mixture of
  cereal grains and oats)
1-1/2 cups whole wheat flour
1 cup wheat germ
1 cup shredded coconut
1 cup chopped nuts
1/2 cup corn meal
1 cup any combination of
  sesame, pumpkin or
  sunflower seeds

1 cup any combination of
  raisins, coarsely chopped
  pitted dates, dried apples
  or dried apricots)
1 tablespoon salt
1 cup honey (or part honey
  and part molasses)
2/3 cup oil
1/2 cup hot water

Mix oats, flour, wheat germ, coconut, nuts, corn meal, seeds, fruit and salt together in a large bowl. In a small bowl, combine honey, oil and hot water. Add honey mixture to grain mixture; spread on cookie sheet. Bake at 225° for 1 hour and 30 minutes; stir every half-hour. Turn off heat and allow mixture to cool in oven; granola will crisp as it cools.

GREAT NUTS

1 egg white
2 tablespoons honey
1 teaspoon salt
1 teaspoon ginger
1/2 teaspoon cinnamon

1/4 teaspoon nutmeg
1/4 teaspoon cloves
2 cups pecan or walnut halves
date sugar

Beat egg white with honey until mixed but not foamy; add seasonings. Stir in nuts; when coated, spread in lightly buttered pan. Sprinkle very lightly with date sugar. Bake at 300° for 30 minutes. Remove from oven; cool slightly. Spread on waxed paper, separating nuts from each other.

MINCEMEAT—UNCOOKED

2 lbs. fresh apples,
   cored and chopped
2 cups unsweetened
   pineapple juice
1 peeled orange, finely
   chopped
2 tablespoons grated
   orange rind
1 lb. raisins
1 lb. currants

1 lb. chopped, pitted dates
1/2 lb. chopped raw almonds
   or pecans
1/4 cup apple juice
2 teaspoons cinnamon
1/2 teaspoon cardamom
1 teaspoon nutmeg
1/2 teaspoon allspice
2 teaspoons vanilla

Mix apples into pineapple juice; add orange rind. Stir in dried fruits and nuts. Mix apple juice and spices in small saucepan; simmer over low heat for 1 minute. Combine juice and fruit mixtures; add vanilla. Allow flavors to develop for 2 to 3 days in refrigerator. Freeze. Remove from freezer and allow to thaw in refrigerator 24 hours before using.

MUNCHIN' CRUNCHIES

1 cup raisins
1 cup sunflower seeds
1 cup granola
3/4 cup chopped walnuts
1/2 cup shelled peanuts

In large bowl, mix ingredients thoroughly. Store in tightly closed container. Change proportions according to your taste. Add dates, coconut, other seeds and nuts as desired.

PARTLY TOASTED TREATS

any quantity seeds or nuts

Place 1/3 of seeds or nuts on cookie sheet. Toast at 300° until barely golden brown. Pour at once into a container with a tightly fitting lid. Add the remaining 2/3 seeds or nuts. Cover container and shake to mix well. Let stand a few hours at room temperature, then store in refrigerator. This method retains nutrients in *most* of the seeds or nuts, while imparting the toasted taste to *all* of them.

SOYBEAN SNACKS

1/4 cup dry soybeans
1 cup cold water
oil and seasonings, if desired

Soak soybeans in water, storing in refrigerator overnight. Drain, dry on clean towel and spread in shallow pan. Roast at 200° for 2 hours; then place under broiler and toast, stirring frequently, until brown. Serve as is or oiled and seasoned.

SUNFLOWER FACES

apple
orange juice
sliced natural cheddar cheese

Core apple and slice into rings. Dip slices into orange juice to keep from turning brown. Make a sandwich of 2 apple rings with a filling of 1 slice of cheese. Serve immediately or wrap and refrigerate for after-school snacks.

TRY-YER-OWN CAROB CHIPS

1 cup water
1/2 cup oil
1 cup honey
2 teaspoons vanilla
1 tablespoon lecithin

1/4 teaspoon salt
1 cup carob powder
1/2 cup soy milk powder
sufficient skim milk powder

Mix together water, oil, honey, vanilla and lecithin. Add, one ingredient at a time, salt, carob powder and soy milk powder. Add just enough skim milk powder to enable mixture to hold together without being sticky. Roll mixture into long, skinny snakes. Let set several hours. Cut into chip-size pieces.

ZINGERS

1 cup pumpkin seeds
1 cup sunflower seeds
1/4 cup sesame seeds
1 tablespoon oil
1 tablespoon soy sauce

1/2 teaspoon cayenne
1/2 teaspoon celery seed
2 teaspoons onion powder
1 teaspoon garlic powder

Mix all ingredients together in large bowl; spread into shallow baking pan. Bake at 300° for 30 minutes; stir every 10 minutes. Cool. Store in airtight container.

MUFFINS

APPLE MUFFINS

1-1/2 cups whole wheat flour
1 teaspoon salt
3 teaspoons baking powder
1-1/2 cups bran
1 teaspoon nutmeg
2 eggs
1/4 cup oil
1/4 cup blackstrap molasses

1/3 cup honey
1-1/2 cups milk
2 tablespoons vinegar
1 teaspoon vanilla
1 teaspoon grated lemon rind
1 cup grated apples
1/2 cup chopped filberts

Combine dry ingredients in large bowl. Set aside. Beat eggs; add oil, molasses, honey, milk, vinegar, vanilla, lemon rind and grated apples. Add apple mixture all at once to dry ingredients. Stir in nuts and mix until just moistened. Fill oiled muffin tins 2/3 full. Bake at 375° for 20 minutes.

BOY SCOUT MUFFINS—
ALWAYS BE PREPARED

2 cups boiling water
6 cups bran
4 eggs
1 cup oil
2 cups honey

5 cups whole wheat flour
4 teaspoons baking powder
1 teaspoon salt
5 cups yoghurt
2 cups chopped, pitted dates

Pour boiling water over bran. Beat eggs; add oil and honey. Add to soaked bran. Stir together flour, baking powder and salt; add to bran mixture alternately with yoghurt. Stir in dates. Fill oiled muffin tins 2/3 full. Bake at 400° for 20 minutes. This batter can be made ahead and stored in tightly covered container in refrigerator for several weeks.

Bran Muffins

1 cup whole wheat flour	1 beaten egg
1 cup bran	1/3 cup milk
3 teaspoons baking powder	1 cup applesauce
1/2 teaspoon salt	1/4 cup oil
2 tablespoons honey	1 teaspoon grated lemon rind

Combine dry ingredients in large bowl. Set aside. Combine remaining ingredients; add all at once to dry ingredients, stirring only until dry ingredients are moistened. Fill oiled muffin tins 2/3 full. Bake at 375° for 20 minutes.

Carrot Muffins

1-1/2 cups whole wheat flour	1/4 cup blackstrap molasses
1 teaspoon salt	1/3 cup honey
3 teaspoons baking powder	1-1/2 cups milk
1-1/2 cups bran	2 tablespoons vinegar
1 teaspoon cinnamon	2 teaspoons grated orange rind
1/2 teaspoon nutmeg	1 cup grated carrots
2 eggs	1/2 cup raisins
1/4 cup oil	

Combine dry ingredients in large bowl. Set aside. Beat eggs; add oil, molasses, honey, milk, vinegar, orange rind and carrots. Add carrot mixture and raisins to dry ingredients; mix until dry ingredients are just moistened. Fill oiled muffin tins 2/3 full. Bake at 375° for 20 minutes.

Cheese Muffins

1 cup cornmeal	1/4 cup oil
1/2 cup whole wheat flour	3 tablespoons honey
1/4 cup soy flour	1 cup milk
1/4 cup wheat germ	1 cup grated natural
2 teaspoons baking powder	cheddar cheese
1/2 teaspoon salt	1/2 cup chopped nuts
1 beaten egg	

Combine cornmeal, flours, wheat germ, baking powder and salt in mixing bowl. Set aside. Mix together egg, oil, honey and milk; add cheese and nuts. Add wet ingredients all at once to dry ingredients; mix just enough to moisten. Fill oiled muffin tins 2/3 full. Bake at 375° for 25 minutes.

DATE MUFFINS

1 cup whole wheat flour
4 teaspoons baking powder
1/4 teaspoon salt
1 cup corn meal
2 eggs

1/4 cup oil
1/4 cup honey
1 cup milk
1 cup chopped, pitted dates

Combine dry ingredients in large bowl. Set aside. Beat eggs; add oil, honey and milk. Add egg mixture all at once to dry ingredients; stir in dates and mix just enough to moisten dry ingredients. Fill oiled muffin tins 2/3 full. Bake at 400° for 20 minutes.

PUMPKIN MUFFINS

2-1/4 cups whole wheat flour
1/2 cup bran
1/4 cup high-protein powder
3 teaspoons baking powder
1 teaspoon cinnamon
1/4 teaspoon cloves
1/2 teaspoon nutmeg
1 teaspoon salt
4 eggs

1/2 cup oil
1 cup honey
1-1/2 cups pumpkin purée
   (see page 13)
1 teaspoon grated orange rind
1 cup raisins
1/2 cup chopped pitted dates
1 cup chopped nuts

Combine flour, bran, protein powder, baking powder, spices and salt in mixing bowl. Set aside. Beat eggs; add oil, honey and pumpkin. Add egg mixture all at once to dry ingredients; add orange rind, raisins, dates and nuts and mix until dry ingredients are just moistened. Fill oiled muffin tins 2/3 full. Bake at 375° for 20 minutes. Allow to cool 5 minutes before removing from pans.

ROMAN MEAL MUFFINS

1/2 cup whole wheat flour
1/2 cup wheat germ
1 teaspoon baking powder
1 teaspoon salt
1 cup Roman Meal

1 egg
3 tablespoons oil
3 tablespoons honey
1 cup milk

Combine flour, wheat germ, baking powder, salt and Roman Meal in mixing bowl. Beat egg; add oil, honey and milk. Add egg mixture all at once to dry ingredients; stir until dry ingredients are just moistened. Fill oiled muffin tins 2/3 full. Bake at 400° for 25 minutes.

ZUCCHINI MUFFINS

1-1/2 cups whole wheat flour
1 teaspoon salt
3 teaspoons baking powder
1-1/2 cups bran
1 teaspoon cinnamon
1/2 teaspoon nutmeg
2 eggs
1/4 cup oil

1/4 cup blackstrap molasses
1/3 cup honey
1-1/2 cups milk
2 tablespoons vinegar
1 teaspoon almond extract
1 cup grated zucchini
1 cup chopped nuts

Combine dry ingredients in large bowl. Set aside. Beat eggs; add oil, molasses, honey, milk, vinegar, almond extract and zucchini. Add zucchini mixture all at once to dry ingredients; add nuts and mix until dry ingredients are just moistened. Fill oiled muffin tins 2/3 full. Bake at 375° for 20 minutes.

PIES & PASTRIES

Coconut Pie Shell

2 tablespoons oil
1-1/2 cups shredded coconut

Spread oil in pie pan; press coconut into oil. If for no-bake filling, prebake shell at 325° for 5 minutes.

Coconut Sesame Crust

1 cup shredded coconut
3/4 cup sesame seeds

Spread coconut and seeds on baking sheet; bake at 300° until lightly browned, stirring occasionally. Pat 1-1/2 cups of mixture into oiled pie pan. Save remainder for sprinkling on top of filling. If for no-bake filling, prebake shell at 325° for 5 minutes.

Coconut Wheaty Crust

1-1/2 cups shredded coconut
1/4 cup wheat germ
1/4 cup bran
2 teaspoons oil

Mix all ingredients together well and press into pie pan. If for no-bake filling, prebake shell at 325° for 5 minutes.

Graham Cracker Crust—Plain

1 cup graham cracker crumbs
1/4 cup melted butter
2 tablespoons honey

Crush crackers with rolling pin or crumb in blender. Mix together melted butter and honey; combine with crumbs. Press into buttered pie pan.

Graham Cracker Crust—Fancy

1 cup graham cracker crumbs
2 tablespoons wheat germ
2 tablespoons bran
1/4 cup oil
2 tablespoons honey

Crush crackers with rolling pin or crumb in blender; mix with wheat germ and bran. Combine oil and honey; add to crumb mixture. Press into pie pan.

Granola Crust

1-1/2 to 2 cups granola (see page 86)
1/4 cup melted butter
soy flour

Lightly crush granola in plastic bag with rolling pin. Place granola in pie pan and drizzle melted butter over it. Press firmly into pan adding soy flour, as needed, to set the crust. If for no-bake filling, prebake shell at 325° for 5 minutes.

High-Protein Crust

3/4 cup wheat germ
1/4 cup bran
2 tablespoons high-protein powder

2 tablespoons sesame seeds
1/4 cup ground nuts
1/4 cup shredded coconut

Mix ingredients together and press 3/4 of the mixture into an oiled pie pan, saving the rest for sprinkling on top of filling. If for no-bake filling, prebake shell at 325° for 5 minutes.

Nut Shell

1-1/2 cups finely ground nuts
1 tablespoon honey
1 tablespoon melted butter

Combine ingredients and press into pie pan. If for no-bake filling, prebake shell at 325° for 5 minutes.

Oat Pie Shell

3/4 cup whole wheat
   pastry flour
3/4 cup rolled oats
1/4 teaspoon salt

1/4 cup toasted sesame seeds
1/2 cup oil
1 tablespoon honey
1/4 cup apple juice (or less)

Combine flour, oats, salt and sesame seeds. Mix oil and honey; slowly cut into flour mixture until it looks like bread crumbs and will stick together when squeezed. Moisten with juice and press into oiled pie pan (the less juice you use, the flakier the crust will be). If for no-bake filling, prebake shell at 375° for 15 to 20 minutes.

Plan-Ahead Pie Crust

1 cup wheat sprouts (see page 7)

Generously butter pie pan and spread sprouts on bottom and sides. If for no-bake filling, prebake shell at 325° for 5 minutes.

Two-Crust Pastry

1-3/4 cups whole wheat
   pastry flour
1/4 cup soy flour

1/2 teaspoon salt
2/3 cup butter
5 to 7 tablespoons ice water

Sift together flours and salt; cut in 1/3 cup butter until the mixture looks like corn meal; cut in the remaining butter until the pieces are the size of small peas. Sprinkle 1 tablespoon water over part of mixture; gently mash with fork and push to one side. Repeat until all is moistened. Form into 2 balls. Place in plastic bag and chill for 15 minutes. Flatten each on lightly floured surface and roll, from center to edge, all directions. Line pie pan with one piece; cover filling with other. If for no-bake filling, line 2 pie pans, prick pastry with fork and prebake at 375° for 15 to 20 minutes.

VINEGAR PASTRY

3 cups whole wheat
   pastry flour
1/2 teaspoon salt
1 teaspoon baking powder
1 beaten egg

1 cup oil
3 tablespoons water
2 tablespoons vinegar
2 tablespoons honey

Sift together flour, salt and baking powder; set aside. Mix together egg, oil, water, vinegar and honey. Add egg mixture to flour; blend with fork. Gather together into ball, place in plastic bag and chill for 15 minutes. Divide dough in half; roll each half between two pieces of waxed paper. If making two bottom crusts for no-bake fillings, prick pastry and prebake at 375° for 15 to 20 minutes or until lightly browned.

WHEAT GERM SPICE CRUST

1 cup wheat germ
1 tablespoon honey
4 tablespoons oil
1/2 teaspoon cinnamon
1/2 teaspoon nutmeg

Combine ingredients and press into pie pan. If for no-bake filling, prebake at 325° for 5 minutes.

WHOLE WHEAT PIE CRUST

1-1/3 cups whole wheat
   pastry flour
1/4 teaspoon salt

1/2 cup chilled butter
1 tablespoon vinegar
4 tablespoons ice water

Combine flour and salt. Cut in butter until mixture looks like corn meal. Mix vinegar and water; sprinkle over flour and blend with fork. Form into a ball. Chill in plastic bag for 15 minutes. Roll chilled dough between two pieces of waxed paper and line pie pan with it. If for no-bake filling, prick bottom with fork and prebake at 375° for 15 to 20 minutes or until lightly browned.

WHOLE WHEAT PRESSED SHELL

1-1/4 cups whole wheat flour
2 tablespoons honey
1/2 cup oil
2 tablespoons milk (or whey)

Combine ingredients and mix well. Pat into ungreased pie pan. If for no-bake filling, prick bottom with fork and prebake at 375° for 15 to 20 minutes.

YOGHURT PASTRY

3-1/2 cups whole wheat
   pastry flour
1/2 teaspoon salt

1/2 cup oil
3 tablespoons yoghurt
2 eggs

Mix flour and salt; stir in oil until mixture resembles coarse bread crumbs. Set aside. Beat yoghurt and eggs together; stir into flour mixture and gather into a ball. Place in plastic bag and chill for 15 minutes. Divide dough in half. Roll each half between two pieces of waxed paper. Line pie pan with one piece; cover filling with other. If for no-bake filling, line 2 pie pans, prick pastry with fork and prebake at 375° for 15 to 20 minutes.

APRICOT PIE

1-1/2 cups dried apricots
3/4 cup honey
1/2 teaspoon lemon rind
1/2 cup water from apricots
1 tablespoon (1 envelope)
  unflavored gelatin
3 slightly beaten egg yolks

1/3 cup (3 oz.) softened
  cream cheese
3 egg whites
2 tablespoons high-protein
  powder
1 cup whipping cream
3 tablespoons honey

1 deep 10-inch crumb pie shell   crumb topping

Cook apricots according to package directions; drain well (save water for softening gelatin). In blender, combine hot apricots, honey and lemon rind; cover and blend until smooth. Place apricot water in saucepan and sprinkle gelatin over it; stir over medium heat until dissolved. Stir some hot apricot mixture into egg yolks; combine with remaining apricot mixture and add this to saucepan. Cook and stir until mixture thickens and boils. Add cream cheese; stir over low heat until well-blended. Cool to room temperature. Beat egg whites until foamy. Add high-protein powder and whip until whites form stiff peaks; fold into apricot mixture. Beat 1/2 cup whipping cream with 1 tablespoon honey until stiff; fold into apricot mixture. Pour into crumb shell. Chill several hours or overnight. Whip remaining cream with 2 tablespoons honey. Top each serving with whipped cream and crumb topping.

BANANA PIE

1 cup hot water
1 tablespoon (1 envelope)
  unflavored gelatin
1/4 cup oil

1 egg
1 teaspoon vanilla
3 bananas

1 baked or crumb pie shell   crumb topping

Combine water and gelatin in blender and process until gelatin is dissolved. Add oil, egg, vanilla and bananas; blend until smooth. Pour into pie shell. Top with crumb topping. Refrigerate several hours or overnight.

BLACK AND WHITE PIE

3 eggs
1/2 cup honey
2 teaspoons vanilla
2 tablespoons high-protein
   powder
1-1/2 cups (12 oz.) softened
   cream cheese

1 cup yoghurt
2 tablespoons honey
1/2 teaspoon almond extract
1/4 cup carob powder
1/2 teaspoon cinnamon

1 pie shell or crumb crust

Beat eggs at high speed until light and frothy. Add honey, vanilla and high-protein powder; beat well. Gradually add cream cheese bits while continuing to whip at medium speed until mixture is very smooth. Pour into pie shell and bake at 375° for 35 minutes or until firm. Cool at room temperature for 30 minutes. Combine yoghurt, honey, almond extract, carob powder and cinnamon and mix until very smooth. Spread carefully on cooled pie (add a ring of crumb topping if you have used crumb crust); bake at 350° for 5 minutes. Refrigerate several hours before serving. For a different taste treat, substitute 1 teaspoon mint extract for the 1/2 teaspoon almond.

BLACKBERRY PIE

1 cup warmed honey
4 cups blackberries
1/4 cup whole wheat flour
3 tablespoons cornstarch

pastry for two-crust pie

Drizzle honey over blackberries. Combine flour and cornstarch; toss with berries. Place berry mixture in pastry-lined pie tin. Add top crust; cut slits for steam. Bake at 400° for 40 to 45 minutes.

CAROB PIE

1/2 cup honey
1/2 cup soy flour
1/3 cup carob powder dissolved
  in 1/2 cup hot water
1/4 teaspoon salt
1-1/2 cups milk

1/4 cup high-protein powder
3 slightly beaten egg yolks
1 tablespoon butter
2 teaspoons vanilla
3 slightly beaten egg whites
1 cup whipping cream

1 pie shell or a crumb crust

Combine honey, flour, carob mix, salt, milk and protein powder in large saucepan. Cook and stir over medium heat until mixture boils and thickens. Cook 2 minutes longer and remove from heat. Add a little of the hot mixture to the egg yolks, then add egg yolks to ingredients in saucepan. Cook 2 minutes longer; remove from heat. Cool slightly before adding butter, then vanilla, and then egg whites. Cool mixture in refrigerator for one hour. Whip and fold in cream and pour into pie shell. Place empty pie plate, upside down, on top of pie for protection. Wrap in foil and freeze. Remove from freezer 1 hour before serving.

CHEERY CHERRY PIE

5 tablespoons cornstarch
1 teaspoon cinnamon
1 cup honey
1/2 teaspoon almond extract

1 cup juice
3-1/2 cups pitted unsweetened
  pie cherries
1 tablespoon butter

pastry for double-crust pie

Mix cornstarch with cinnamon. Mix honey with fruit juice. Combine juice mixture and cornstarch mixture in saucepan; cook and stir over medium heat until mixture thickens and clears. Stir in almond extract and cherries. Pour into pastry-lined pie pan, dot with butter, add top crust and cut slits. Bake at 425° for 45 minutes.

Coconut Creme Pie

1 cup (8 oz.) cream cheese
2/3 cup yoghurt
2 tablespoons honey

1 teaspoon vanilla
1-1/4 cups shredded coconut

1 pie shell

Blend together cream cheese, yoghurt, honey and vanilla. Fold in coconut, reserving one tablespoon for topping. Pour into pie shell; top with reserved coconut. Chill until set. For a special taste treat, add 1/2 cup chopped pitted dates with the coconut.

Cool Fruit Pie

1 tablespoon (1 envelope)
  unflavored gelatin
1/2 cup juice or water
1/2 cup honey
juice of 1/2 lemon

1/4 teaspoon almond extract
1-1/4 cups mashed or sliced
  fresh berries or fruit
1 cup whipping cream

1 pie shell

Sprinkle gelatin over juice in saucepan; cook and stir over medium heat until gelatin is dissolved. Stir in honey, lemon juice and almond extract; add fruit and cook until mixture thickens. Cool. Whip cream into soft peaks; fold into cooled fruit mixture. Pour into pie shell and refrigerate several hours before serving.

Creamy Carrot Pie

2 cups mashed, cooked carrots
1/2 teaspoon salt
3/4 cup heavy cream
2 eggs

1/2 cup honey
1 tablespoon oil
1 tablespoon pumpkin pie spice
1 teaspoon vanilla

1 unbaked pie shell

Beat together carrots, salt, cream, eggs, honey, oil, spice and vanilla. Pour into pie shell; bake at 375° for 45 minutes.

A HONEY OF A CHEESE PIE

2 cups (16 oz.) softened
  cream cheese

3 eggs
1/2 cup honey

1 unbaked crumb crust
2 cups yoghurt

3 tablespoons honey
1 teaspoon vanilla

Whip cheese with mixer; add eggs and honey and beat until smooth. Pour into pie shell; bake at 325° for 30 minutes. Cool. Combine yoghurt, 3 tablespoons honey and vanilla and spread over cooled cheese pie. Return to oven, baking at 475° for 5 minutes. Cool. Refrigerate.

JOG APPLE PIE

2 tablespoons whole wheat
  pastry flour
1 cup yoghurt
1/2 teaspoon nutmeg
1/4 teaspoon salt

1 teaspoon vanilla
1/2 cup honey
1 unbeaten egg
2 cups diced apples

1 unbaked pie shell

crumb topping

Beat all ingredients except apples, pie shell and crumb topping into a thin paste. Stir in apples; pour into pie shell. Bake at 400° for 15 minutes, then 350° for 30 minutes. Remove from oven and sprinkle with crumb topping. Return to oven for 5 minutes.

MAPLE PIE

2 well-beaten eggs
2/3 cup rolled oats
1/3 cup oil

2/3 cup maple syrup
1/4 teaspoon salt
1 teaspoon vanilla

unbaked pie shell

Mix together eggs, rolled oats, oil, maple syrup, salt and vanilla. Pour into shell. Place in preheated 350° oven; reduce temperature at once to 300°. Bake for 35 minutes.

Mincemeat Pie

1 tablespoon (1 envelope)
   unflavored gelatin
1/2 cup water
6 tablespoons honey
1/4 cup rum or 1 tablespoon
   rum flavoring (optional)

1-1/2 cups mincemeat
3 egg whites
1/8 teaspoon salt
1 cup whipping cream

1 baked pie shell

Sprinkle gelatin over water in saucepan; stir over low heat until dissolved. Stir in honey, rum and mincemeat. Chill until mixture mounds slightly when dropped from spoon. Beat egg whites until stiff, but not dry. Add salt and beat until very stiff. Fold into gelatin mixture. Whip and fold in cream. Pour into baked shell; chill until firm. If desired, garnish with additional whipped cream sprinkled with crumb topping.

Peach Pie

3/4 cup warm honey
5 cups sliced fresh peaches
4 tablespoons whole wheat flour
2 tablespoons butter

pastry for double-crust pie

Drizzle honey over peaches; sprinkle flour over peaches and toss to coat evenly. Place mixture in pastry-lined pie pan; dot with butter. Add top crust; cut slits to allow steam to escape. Bake at 425° for 35 to 45 minutes.

Pecan Pie

2 cups pecan halves
1 unbaked pie shell
4 eggs
1 cup honey
1 teaspoon vanilla

Spread pecans in pie shell. Beat together eggs, honey and vanilla; pour over nuts. Bake at 375° for 30 minutes. Reduce temperature to 325° and bake 30 minutes longer or until puffed and set.

POLLIWOG PIE

2 tablespoons honey
 (adjust to taste)
1/4 teaspoon salt
1-1/2 cups fruit juice

1 tablespoon (1 envelope)
 unflavored gelatin
1/2 cup whipping cream
3 stiffly beaten egg whites

1 baked pie shell

Mix honey, salt and juice in saucepan. Sprinkle gelatin over this. Heat and stir over low heat until dissolved. Cool until mixture mounds when dropped from spoon. Whip and fold in cream; fold in egg whites. Pour into pie shell. Chill several hours until set.

PRUNE PIE

2 cups cooked prunes
3 tablespoons honey
1 teaspoon ground orange rind

1/2 teaspoon cinnamon
4 egg whites

1 unbaked pie shell

Remove pits from prunes. Mash prunes or process in blender (1 cup at a time) with honey, orange rind and cinnamon. Beat egg whites until stiff; fold into prune mixture. Pile lightly into pie shell. Bake at 350° for 20 to 30 minutes.

PUMPKIN PIE

2 cups puréed cooked pumpkin
(see page 13)
2 tablespoons butter
1 cup honey
1 teaspoon cinnamon

1 teaspoon nutmeg
1/2 cup orange juice
1 teaspoon ground orange rind
3 eggs, separated
1 cup yoghurt

1 unbaked pie shell

Beat together pumpkin, butter, honey, cinnamon, nutmeg, orange juice, orange rind, yoghurt and egg yolks. Beat egg whites until stiff and fold into pumpkin mixture. Pour into pie shell; bake at 350° for 35 to 45 minutes.

RAISIN PIE

2 cups raisins
1-1/2 cups juice or water
6 tablespoons honey
(or to taste)
3 tablespoons whole wheat flour

1/2 cup chopped nuts
3 tablespoons lemon juice
1 teaspoon ground lemon rind

pastry for double-crust pie

Cook raisins and juice in covered pan for 10 minutes or until raisins are plumped. Stir in honey, sprinkle in flour and cook over low heat, stirring constantly, until mixture thickens and bubbles. Cook 1 minute more. Remove from heat. Stir in nuts, lemon juice and lemon rind. Roll out bottom crust, put in pie pan and pour in filling. Roll out top crust, place over filling and seal crusts together. Cut slits in top crust to allow steam to escape. Bake at 425° for 30 to 40 minutes. If edge of crust browns too quickly, cover with foil strip.

SWEET POTATO SWEETIE PIE

1-1/2 cups mashed cooked
  sweet potatoes
3 tablespoons oil
1/2 cup honey
3 eggs, separated

dash salt
1 teaspoon cinnamon
1/3 cup chopped almonds
1-1/2 cups nut milk

1 unbaked pie shell

Combine sweet potatoes, oil and honey. Beat egg yolks; add salt and cinnamon and mix thoroughly with potato mixture. Combine almonds and nut milk; add to mixture. Beat egg whites until stiff and fold in. Pour into pie shell. Bake at 425° for 15 minutes; reduce temperature to 375° and bake 25 minutes more.

TWO-TONE PUNK

1 cup (8 oz.) softened
  cream cheese
1/4 cup honey
1 teaspoon vanilla
1 egg
deep 9-inch unbaked pie shell
1-1/4 cups cooked pumpkin
  (see page 13)

1/3 cup honey
1 teaspoon cinnamon
1/4 teaspoon each ginger,
  nutmeg, cloves, salt
2 slightly beaten eggs
1 cup cream (or 1 cup milk
  into which 1/3 cup powdered
  milk has been blended)

Beat cream cheese in bowl; add honey, vanilla and egg. Mix well. Spread on the bottom of pie shell. Mix pumpkin and honey with spices and salt. Blend in eggs and cream. Carefully pour over the cheese mixture. Bake at 350° for 65 to 70 minutes.

YUMMY YAMMY

1/2 cup powdered milk
1/2 teaspoon each salt, ginger,
  cinnamon, cloves
1-1/2 cups mashed
  cooked yams

3 beaten eggs
1-1/4 cups juice or water
1/4 cup honey
1 tablespoon molasses
1 teaspoon vanilla

1 unbaked pie shell

Mix together dry ingredients. Combine yams, eggs, juice, honey, molasses and vanilla and add to dry ingredients. Pour into pie shell. Bake at 450° for 10 minutes; reduce temperature to 350° and bake 30 minutes more.

BASIC BERRY COBBLER

4 cups berries
1/2 cup honey (adjust to taste)
2 tablespoons cornstarch
1 tablespoon oil
2 teaspoons lemon juice

Mix berries, honey and cornstarch in saucepan; stir over medium heat until thickened and clear. Stir in oil and lemon juice. Pour into oiled 8-inch square baking dish. Finish by following topping recipe (see page 114).

BASIC FRUIT COBBLER

3 cups sliced fresh fruit
3/4 cup honey (adjust to taste)
1 tablespoon lemon juice

spices or flavoring
for apples: 1 teaspoon cinnamon
                1 teaspoon nutmeg
for peaches: 1/2 teaspoon almond extract
for pears: 1 teaspoon nutmeg
                1/2 teaspoon ginger

Arrange sliced fruit in oiled 8-inch square baking pan; drizzle mixture of honey, lemon juice and appropriate spices or flavoring over fruit. Heat at 200° until just hot while preparing topping (see below).

COBBLER TOPPING

1 cup whole wheat flour
2 tablespoons soy flour
1/4 cup bran
2 tablespoons high-protein
  powder
1 tablespoon baking powder
1/4 teaspoon salt
1 beaten egg
1/2 cup milk
1 tablespoon oil

Whisk together flours, bran, protein powder, baking powder and salt. Set aside. Mix egg, milk and oil. Add to flour mixture; mix until dry ingredients are just moistened. Drop by tablespoonfuls onto hot fruit or berry mixture. Bake at 375° for approximately 30 minutes or until lightly browned.

APPLE CRISP—PLAIN

3 to 5 tart apples
1/4 cup raisins
1/4 cup chopped nuts
1 teaspoon cinnamon
1 teaspoon nutmeg
1/2 cup rolled oats
1/2 cup bran

1/2 cup wheat germ
1/4 cup soy flour
1/4 cup high-protein powder
1/2 cup oil
1/2 cup honey
whipping cream
honey

Place peeled, sliced apples in oiled baking dish; sprinkle with raisins, nuts, cinnamon and nutmeg. Combine oats, bran, wheat germ, soy flour and protein powder. Combine oil and honey. Combine oat and honey mixtures; distribute evenly over the top of apples. Bake at 350° for approximately 30 minutes. Serve with whipped cream sweetened with honey.

APPLE CRISP—NUTTY

3 to 5 tart apples
1/2 teaspoon ground lemon rind
2 tablespoons lemon juice
1 teaspoon nutmeg
1/2 cup chopped pitted dates
1/2 cup rolled oats
1/2 cup wheat germ
1/2 cup bran

1/4 cup high-protein powder
1/2 cup peanut butter
1/4 cup honey
1/4 cup oil
whipping cream
honey
almond extract

Place peeled, sliced apples in oiled baking dish; sprinkle with lemon rind and juice, nutmeg and dates. Combine oats, wheat germ, bran and protein powder. Combine peanut butter, oil and honey. Combine oat and peanut butter mixtures; distribute evenly over the top of apples. Bake at 350° for approximately 30 minutes. Serve plain or with whipped cream sweetened with honey and flavored with almond extract.

HEARTY PIE

A little different pie...for the teenagers after the game, maybe.

Crust:

1/2 cup short grain brown rice
1 cup boiling water

Wash rice; drain and place in heavy saucepan. Stir over medium heat until grains are dry. Add boiling water. Cover and barely simmer over low heat until water has been absorbed and rice is thoroughly steamed (30 to 45 minutes). Pat slightly cooled rice on the bottom and sides of a lightly buttered pie plate. Bake at 375° for 5 minutes to dry but not brown the crust. Remove from oven and cool before adding filling.

Cheddar Filling:

1/2 cup chopped onion
1 clove crushed garlic
2 cups grated natural cheddar
3/4 cup yoghurt

1 cup diced cooked meat
2 slightly beaten eggs
1/4 teaspoon salt

Lightly sauté onion and garlic. Combine all ingredients and place in brown rice shell. Bake at 375° for 25 to 30 minutes or until a knife inserted half way between the center and the rim comes out clean.

SHORTCAKE

1-1/2 cups whole wheat flour
1/2 cup arrowroot powder
2 teaspoons baking powder
1/2 teaspoon salt

1/4 cup butter
3/4 cup milk
fruit
whipping cream

Stir together flour, arrowroot powder, baking powder and salt. Cut in butter until coarse crumbs form. Mix in milk with fork just until ball forms. Gently knead on lightly floured surface. Roll to 1/2-inch thickness. Cut with lightly floured 2-1/2-inch biscuit cutter (an empty tuna can will work) and place on ungreased baking sheet. Bake at 450° for 15 to 20 minutes until lightly browned. Break apart while warm (not hot) and serve with fruit and whipped cream.

TURNOVERS

pastry for single-crust pie
3/4 cup pared, cored
  and diced apples
1/4 cup chopped pitted dates

3 tablespoons honey
1/4 teaspoon nutmeg
1 tablespoon butter

Roll pastry dough 1/8-inch thick. Cut into 5-inch squares. Combine apples and dates. Drizzle honey over fruit and sprinkle with nutmeg. Toss lightly. Put 2 tablespoons fruit mixture in center of each pastry square. Dot with butter. Dampen edges of pastry with water; fold each square diagonally. Press edges together with floured fork. Prick tops to allow steam to escape. Bake on ungreased baking sheet at 450° for 15 to 20 minutes.

SAUCES AND SPREADS

Avocado-Banana Dip/Spread

1 mashed ripe banana
1 pitted and mashed
  ripe avocado
1 teaspoon lemon juice
1/4 cup finely ground
  wheat germ

1/4 cup finely chopped
  seeds or nuts
1/4 cup orange juice
  (for dip)

Blend all ingredients well and use for dip. Omit orange juice and use for spread.

Caramel Dip/Spread

1/4 cup molasses
1/4 cup peanut butter
1/2 cup wheat germ
1/4 cup apple juice

Blend ingredients for dip. Omit apple juice and use for spread.

Cottage Dip

1 cup cottage cheese
6 tablespoons (3 oz.)
  cream cheese
2 tablespoons mayonnaise
  (see page 9)

2 tablespoons milk
1 clove garlic
1/2 teaspoon cayenne
1/4 cup chopped chives
parsley and salt to taste

Process ingredients in blender until smooth. Refrigerate several hours or overnight before serving.

CREAM CHEESE DIP/SPREAD

1 cup (8 oz.) cream cheese
1/4 cup orange juice
finely chopped nuts

Moisten cream cheese with orange juice and add finely chopped nuts for dip. Decrease amount of orange juice to 2 tablespoons and use for spread.

NUTSY DIP/SPREAD

3/4 cup tahini
  (sesame seed butter)
1/2 cup almond, peanut
  or other nut butter
  (see page 9)

1/2 cup finely chopped
  sunflower, pumpkin or
  sesame seeds
1 tablespoon honey
1/4 cup apple juice

Blend ingredients for dip. Omit apple juice for spread.

QUICK SPREAD

honey
butter or peanut butter
finely chopped nuts or seeds

Spread mixture of honey and butter or honey and peanut butter on slices of dessert bread; sprinkle with nuts or seeds. Broil until bubbly.

SESAME CHEESE DIP/SPREAD

1 cup grated cheese
2 tablespoons oil
2 tablespoons yoghurt
1/2 cup partly toasted
  sesame seeds (page 88)

1/2 teaspoon salt
3 tablespoons finely chopped
  chives, dill or parsley

Blend with wooden spoon for spread; add 1/2 cup more yoghurt for dip.

BASIC CREAM CHEESE FROSTING
WITH VARIATIONS

1 cup (8 oz.) softened cream cheese
2 tablespoons honey (or to taste)
2 tablespoons whipping cream
2 tablespoons high-protein powder

Blend ingredients well with mixer until mixture is the consistency of your choice.

For variations:
...add anise flavoring and sprinkle with poppy seeds
...add mint extract and decorate with carob chips
...substitute lemon juice for cream; add almond extract
...substitute orange juice for cream; add vanilla
...substitute berry juice for cream; add peppermint extract
...substitute 2 tablespoons carob powder for 2 tablespoons high-protein powder

BASIC BERRY OR FRUIT SAUCE

3 tablespoons cornstarch
1 cup juice
honey to taste

1 cup mashed, sliced, diced
or whole tidbits of fruit
flavorings as desired

Dissolve cornstarch in 3 tablespoons juice; pour it and remaining juice into saucepan; add honey. Stir over medium heat until mixture thickens, bubbles and clears. Add fruit; cook 2 minutes. Remove from heat and add flavorings.

CARAMEL SAUCE

3 to 4 tablespoons cornstarch
2 cups juice (or water)
1 cup molasses
1/4 cup butter
1 teaspoon almond extract

In saucepan, dissolve cornstarch in 3 tablespoons juice; add remaining juice, molasses and butter. Stir over medium heat until mixture thickens, bubbles and clears. Remove from heat and add almond extract.

CAROB SAUCE

3 natural or mint carob candy bars
   (4 oz. each); check label to be certain
   they contain no unwanted ingredients
1 cup milk

Melt candy bars in 1/2 cup milk in top of double boiler. When melted, add remaining milk and stir until smooth and glossy. May be stored in the refrigerator for 2 weeks. Before using, thin with additional milk or warm by placing in bowl of warm water.

HONEY-BUTTER SAUCE

3 to 4 tablespoons cornstarch
2 cups juice (or water)
1 cup honey
1/4 cup butter
2 teaspoons vanilla

In saucepan dissolve cornstarch in 3 tablespoons juice; add remaining juice, honey and butter. Stir over medium heat until mixture thickens, bubbles and clears. Remove from heat and add vanilla.

"SOFT" DRINKS

Apple Pie 'n Ice Cream Shake

1 cup milk
1 cut-up apple
1 teaspoon vanilla
1 tablespoon high-protein
  powder

1/2 teaspoon cinnamon
1/4 teaspoon allspice
1/4 teaspoon nutmeg
2 cracked ice cubes

Process in blender until foamy.

Banana Cooler

4 ripe bananas
1/4 cup freshly squeezed
  lemon juice
1 cup vanilla ice cream

3 tablespoons honey
  (or to taste)
dash salt
1 cup yoghurt

Peel and slice bananas; soak slices in lemon juice 5 minutes. Reserve a couple of slices for garnish. Place bananas, juice and all other ingredients into blender and process until smooth and frothy.

Berry Froth

1 cup berries
1 cup vanilla ice cream
1 tablespoon honey (or to taste)
1 cracked ice cube

Save a couple of berries for garnish. Put all other ingredients into blender and process until smooth and frothy.

"COFFEE"

garbanzos (chickpeas), sunflower seeds,
   whole feed barley (not cracked grain
   or seed barley, since insecticides are
   often added to these) or oats

Roast grain or seeds on a baking sheet at 500° for approximately 30 minutes or until dry and very dark brown. Stir occasionally and check often. When cool, put through grinder or mill; grind coarsely, like coffee, and brew 1 tablespoon per cup. If you like your "coffee" sweetened, try honey.

CRANBERRY-APPLE JUICE

1-1/2 cups fresh apple juice
1/2 cup cranberries

Put 1 cup juice and all the cranberries in blender and process until berries are puréed; add remaining juice and mix. Let juice stand a few minutes to extract the color and flavor from the cranberries. Strain or use with cranberry bits.

CRANBERRY BLEND

1 cup yoghurt
2 tablespoons honey (or to taste)
1 cup cranberries
1 tablespoon wheat germ
1 tablespoon high-protein powder

Place ingredients in blender and process until smooth.

Date Shake

1 egg
1 cup chopped pitted dates
1 cut-up ripe banana
2 tablespoons honey
   (or to taste)

2 cups milk
1/4 teaspoon salt
1 teaspoon vanilla
2 tablespoons high-protein
   powder

Process egg and dates in blender until smooth. Add banana, honey and 1/2 cup milk; process again until smooth. Add remaining ingredients and blend.

Eggnog

1 egg
1 cup milk
1 tablespoon high-protein
   powder

1/2 teaspoon vanilla
1/2 teaspoon almond extract
1/2 teaspoon nutmeg

Process ingredients in blender until smooth and creamy. For variety, add 2 tablespoons carob powder (Carob Eggnog).

Fruit Smoothie

1/2 cup fruit juice
1 cut-up apple
1 ripe banana

1/2 cup other cut-up fruit
1 tablespoon high-protein
   powder

Process ingredients in blender until very smooth and frothy.

Liquid Lunch

1 cup apple juice
1/2 cup orange juice
1 tablespoon raisins
3/4 cup almonds
1/4 cup diced carrots
1 small diced celery stalk
2 sprigs parsley

2 leaves spinach or
   romaine lettuce
1/2 cup diced apple
1 small banana
1 egg
2 tablespoons high-protein
   powder

Process ingredients in blender until well-blended and smooth. Add cracked ice and process again. Can go with you in a Thermos.

MELLOW COOLER

1 cup milk
1 tablespoon molasses
  (or to taste)
1 tablespoon high-protein
  powder

4 pitted dates, figs, prunes
  or 1/4 cup raisins

Process ingredients in blender until smooth and creamy.

PEACHY PICK-ME-UP

1 fresh peach
5 pitted dates
1 banana
1 peeled orange

2 tablespoons honey
  (or to taste)
1 cup apple juice

Place cut-up fruit, honey and juice in blender. Process until smooth.

YELLOW SUBMARINE

1/2 cup lemon juice
1/2 cup unsweetened
  pineapple juice
1 tablespoon honey (or to taste)

1 egg
1 tablespoon high-protein
  powder

Process ingredients in blender until smooth and frothy.

Yoghurt Yummy

1 cup yoghurt

2 tablespoons wheat germ

4 tablespoons shredded coconut

1 banana

2 tablespoons high-protein powder

2 cups unsweetened pineapple juice

Process ingredients in blender until smooth and creamy.

INDEX